HOW TO RUN *& Run* A

SUCCESSFUL MULTI-DISCIPLINARY

DESIGN COMPANY

BY

MARCELLO MINALE

A special thanks to:
Liza Honey
Julia Williams
Evelyn Hegi
Michael Callan
for helping me 'put together' this book.

Front cover illustration by Marcello Minale.

Published by:
Internos Books
12 Percy Street
London W1P 9FB
Tel: 0171 637 4255 Fax: 0171 637 4251
ISBN 1873968795

Italian distributor:
Ulrico Hoepli Editore Spa
20121 Milano Via Hoepli 5
Tel: (02) 86 4871 Fax: (02) 805 2885
ISBN 8820322781

Printed in Singapore by Toppan Printing Co (S) Pte. Ltd.

Thank you to ALL
including the EX
at Minale, Tattersfield
Design Strategy ......
Without their CREATIVE
talent and support
this book could'nt
have been written....

Morello
London 1966
7

The famous symbol of:
Minale, Tattersfield Design Strategy Group
International Design Consultants
The Courtyard
37 Sheen Road
Richmond
Surrey TW9 1AJ ENGLAND
Telephone: 0181 948 7999 Fax: 0181 948 2435
ISDN: 0181 332 2160 E-mail: mintat@cityscape.co.uk.
Website: http://www.mintat.co.uk

Offices in: London, Paris, Milan, Brussels, Hamburg, Zürich, Prague, Oslo, Casablanca, Kuwait, Jeddah, Kuala Lumpur, Hong Kong, Osaka, Tokyo, Brisbane, Sydney.

CONTENTS

INTRODUCTION
By Jeremy Myerson

INTRODUCTION

BY JEREMY MYERSON

When Marcello Minale's highly entertaining and unorthodox account of how to set up, survive and succeed in running a multi-disciplinary design consultancy was first published in 1991, this outspoken book caused an immediate stir in the design industry.

Here was a respected commentator – a veteran of the initial development of the British design business in the early 1960s – who was not afraid to tell it like it is. From the courting of clients and the struggles with cash-flow to the secrets of how to retain staff, attract publicity and build an international business, Minale's swashbuckling, warts-and-all insight into how he and partner Brian Tattersfield established one of the world's best known design firms caught the imagination.

The book raced to the top of the Design Centre Bookshop bestsellers list within two months of publication. Critics praised its fresh and direct tone. In *Design Review*, Michael Wolff described it as "a personal and idiosyncratic tale about the Minale Tattersfield philosophy...an honest and useful book." In *Design*, Marion Hancock observed that "Minale has no pretensions to management-speak. On the contrary he rejects the idea that long-term planning has a place in the running of a design consultancy."

Such sentiments clearly struck a chord and letters from readers began to pour in from around the world. Venus Lee of Magic Kingdom Advertising and Production in Hong Kong summed up the feeling: "The book reminds me of why I've been working so hard for the past 10 years and reminds me of my dreams for my career path....you are my mentor."

What Marcello Minale wrote was no conventional biography detailing past exploits. It was written to provide designers at all levels – from aspiring students to established design consultants – with a wealth of information and insight into how to avoid the pitfalls and realise their own and their colleagues' potential.

Now, five years after the success of the sell-out first edition, Minale has returned to update the book with two completely new chapters which bring the story right up to the hour. He addresses the two biggest structural changes in the global design industry in the 1990s – economic recession and new technology – and once again provides forthright views on how to survive and prosper.

His account of how Minale Tattersfield hung on in the recession is a hair-raising tale of taking chances on new markets and opportunities amid unprecedented financial, social and economic turmoil. It shows that even when luck deserts you, the designer's skill in lateral thinking can still find a way through. The chapter on Minale Tatterfield's decision to move into interactive communications opens up a significant debate on the future of design creativity in the digital era – a talking point which will affect every designer in the future.

As with earlier chapters, much of Marcello Minale's advice runs counter to the prevailing wisdom within the design industry. He suggests that the recession was actually a good thing for the design business because it made it leaner, fitter and stronger in spirit. And he predicts that multimedia could be a gigantic market flop – an answer to a problem that doesn't exist.

Taken as a whole, this new, revised edition of *How To Run and Run A Successful Multi-Disciplinary Design Company* reaffirms Marcello Minale as a champion of a broader, more cultural, problem-solving approach to design, rather than a servant of marketing – and as a humanist in design who believes that human talent and imagination provide far better guarantees for our future than any amount of clever machines.

Jeremy Myerson is a design writer and critic, author of a number of books, and a contributor to newspapers and magazines all over the world. He is Professor of Contemporary Design at De Montfort University. He also founded the world's first weekly design magazine, Design Week, and is a former editor of Creative Review. He has a Masters degree from the Royal College of Art.

Marcello Minale, attempting to prove that he can ride on water, in this case during the Oxford and Cambridge boat race, Putney, April 1994.

CHAPTER ONE

FIRST STEPS – GAINING THE RIGHT EXPERIENCE

GAINING THE RIGHT EXPERIENCE

The road to running your own successful multi-disciplinary design company doesn't start the day you set up your own business. It doesn't even start the day you leave college with a design qualification. It starts while you are still being educated, soaking up the experiences and the influences which will shape your future direction as a designer.

The chain is a well-formed one: the subjects you learn, the ideas you explore and the contacts you make while still in an educational environment, which allows you the luxury of making mistakes and falling flat on your face with a certain modicum of grace, will have a great bearing in the short term on that all-important first job as a graduate and in the long term on the career path you eventually carve out.

I won't pretend that luck or chance doesn't play a large role in the destiny of the designer who chooses to combine professional practice with that element of entrepreneurship necessary to survive at the head of a design consultancy. Fate has certainly intervened unexpectedly at several stages in my own career, as this book will demonstrate. You can't legislate for every eventuality and it would be an unimaginative designer who wanted to do so. External pressure from an unpredicted source can be a wonderful creative stimulus. But if you genuinely believe – and many design students clearly do – that your goal is to run your own design company, then there are certain measures you can take which go some way to help you achieve your ambition.

1991: Prospectus and annual report for the West Surrey College of Art and Design. Designed by Minale Tattersfield.

Chief among these is getting the right education. I am often asked what that means. It means a classical education which has an academic breadth and a cultural depth to encourage the development of those all-important intellectual skills to enable the designer to analyse problems, devise intelligent solutions and communicate those solutions to others. That, in essence, is what being a designer is all about.

TAKING THE BROADER VIEW

In the great debate between a narrow vocational design training which produces the hired studio hand versus a broader, more cultural education which shapes the designer who can think, I firmly believe in the latter. That way the educational process is more intangible and harder to manage and assess, but the results are worth the effort because you need a broadness of vision to be a designer, and especially to run a multi-disciplinary design consultancy which involves constant mental contortions. In the course of any day, you will be forced to make the intellectual and practical leap from one subject to another maybe 20 times. You could begin the day by looking at how a logo works on a letterhead, and end it by assessing the wheel bearings of a high-speed train.

For that reason, the problem solving aspect of designing assumes great importance. It has certainly influenced the type of designer I employ. At Minale Tattersfield, we have tended over the years to take graduates directly from the Royal College of Art, Norwich School of Art and Kingston Polytechnic precisely because these colleges produce problem solvers who are aware of the broader

Brian Tattersfield designed this while still at the Royal College of Art: 1960.

picture. So whatever course you are on, try to take the broader view and be aware of what the design profession offers. Listen closely to your tutors and any part-time visiting lecturers; look around, read the trade magazines and, wherever possible, visit design exhibitions. Ignorance isn't bliss so far as design is concerned, just a gigantic wasted opportunity.

Get to know the names of design consultancies, and what they specialise in. Try to match up your own interests – these will be forming strongly by your final year, whether corporate identity, book and record sleeves, street furniture or hi-fi equipment – to potential employers in the field. The design market is full of niches and niche players. Set your sights. If you eventually want to run your own design business, then the best way to start is by getting a good job in a respected and significant design group where you can observe how things are done and learn how to do them properly.

Above all, don't take the first job offer that comes along just because it is there. You need to get off on the right footing if you want to make a success of your career. Rightly or wrongly, the design industry is built on fashionable reputation and it is better to hold out for a job with a more prestigious or charismatic design company capable of building bridges for you into the future than taking the easy option with a firm with a bad reputation doing poor work. I realise that this is hard advice to swallow given the perennially high levels of unemployment among design graduates. But jobs which are easy to come by are often that way for all the wrong reasons. If you want to be true to your ambition to be a top-flight design consultant, then you should hold out for the right position which will give you the necessary experience and reputation you need to strike out on your own in the long term.

TARGETING LIKELY EMPLOYERS

You can, of course, take pre-emptive action to pre-select the jobs you go up for. As part of your research of the design market as a student, target ten firms you'd like to work for. Write to them well ahead of graduation and try to fix up a work placement during vacations. These can sometimes lead to full employment. But don't offer your services for free as some misguided students do. It is demeaning to both applicant and employer. One of my most fervently held beliefs is that nobody in design should do work for nothing. That applies as much to students on placement as design firms preparing speculative creative ideas for unpaid business pitches.

You should also take every opportunity to get out and personally meet potential employers in the design world. Workshops and seminars run by such institutions as D&AD or the Chartered Society of Designers, at which leading designers lecture or set and assess projects, are ideal forums to make contact and make an impression.

It is a truism but the more people you meet at an early stage, the more chance you will have to make headway in the design profession. You can, however, blow it if your attempt to impress your peers strikes the wrong note. I well remember my own student days when the American guru of graphic design, Bob Gill, came to the Royal College of Art to give a guest lecture. His

MARCELLO FERN
GERT MINALE
DAN DUMBAR

THE GRAPHIC WORKSHOP
SPONSORED BY THE DESIGNERS & ART DIRECTORS ASSOCIATION

A series of 'call for entry' posters for the D&AD Graphic Workshop 1970 - 73.
We have tried to express the mental challenge of problem solving.

presentation was electrifying: brilliant creative solutions delivered at breakneck speed. When he was finished, he asked his dazzled audience for questions. One earnest scholar out to impress immediately put his hand up. "What about international paper sizes?" he asked. "What about it," snapped an exasperated Gill and walked out.

SURVIVING THE INTERVIEW

The question I always ask myself when confronted by potential Minale Tattersfield designers at interview stage is: if I scratch the surface, is there something underneath? By that, I mean that applicants must demonstrate that their design work goes beyond superficial presentation to reflect a degree of thinking. That thinking doesn't have to be at all logical, but there should be a semblance of logic in the illogicality – if that isn't impossible.

I also, quite seriously, look at interviewees' shoes. Shoes are an important indication of inner character: you cannot wear the wrong shoes, it is such a personal choice. When I visited Australia, I was alarmed to find that so many young designers wore a certain make of grey shoes. This puzzled me, then I discovered that if you bought a suit you got a pair of grey shoes thrown in for free. That reflected badly on the quality of designers in the Land of Oz as far as I was concerned.

I also look for designers with outside interests. If young designers are too obsessed with design, that is worrying: how can they see the wood for the trees? They need external stimuli. A love of needlework won't necessarily impress me but an active involvement in sport will. Why? I believe that people who play sport are honest with themselves because of the need to compete within rules. And at the end of day, design is all about honesty – about honestly knowing whether something is good or bad. Out of that honesty about a design springs the conviction to sell it to clients or communicate it to colleagues effectively.

On the strength of this excellent piece of work, Ray Gregory (RCA) was offered a job at Minale Tattersfield in 1972.

New graduates should also act their age. Their chief asset is immaturity, freshness, *joie de vie*. They shouldn't be old before their time or too serious about the design business. It may be a great business to be in but one shouldn't take it too seriously. An element of fun, innocence, craziness even, should always be maintained. Picasso did more outrageous work at the end of his life than in his early thirties.

What I call perfect work (wish I'd done it!) by Kate Emamooden: Norwich School of Art, 1990.

In this context, creative communication with a potential employer should be considered. New graduates try lots of tricks. I have heard of 48-sheet self-advertising posters fly-posted to walls opposite the front entrance of the design studio and spoof grocery hampers delivered with CVs attached. Many stunts backfire but sometimes they can work quite spectacularly.

A student recently came to see Minale Tattersfield. Afterwards he sent us a card with the single word *Thanks* written on it in the style of the consultancy's corporate mark, The Scribble. This card is one of the nicest creative gestures I've received in 25 years in business. It was well executed and shrewdly judged:

if he'd written a whole page in Scribble-style, that would have been over the top, but the single word is a perfect solution. Its simplicity, wit and clarity of thought epitomises Minale Tattersfield's belief in what constitutes good design. And it came from a student.

A nice way to say thanks after an interview at Minale Tattersfield. A 'scribble' of thanks from Greg Quinton, in the style of our logo, said it all: 1990.

DESIGNING YOUR PORTFOLIO

The stiffest hurdle for any new graduate to overcome is in presenting a portfolio which shows your talents to the best advantage. It requires you to be self-critical, to step back, to leave material out, *to show judgement.* Your success in overcoming this hurdle will go some way to determining your suitability to one day run your own design firm, when judgement will be all.

My personal view is that a brilliant portfolio can have just one job in it and still be a brilliant portfolio provided that job is really good. My definition of a good job is "I wish I'd done that!" This is usually when the concept is fine, the idea is strong, the implementation faultless and the presentation perfect. If you have such a job, then let it shine by allowing it to stand out in company with maybe two or three others. Don't cram your portfolio with 20 mediocre jobs because the one really good solution will get lost in their midst. Employers will also think that the one good job is a fluke or a happy accident, given the extent of accompanying dross. We've all done lousy jobs in our time. The skill is in recognising the fact and the judgement is in knowing what to leave out. When it comes to portfolios, less is more.

There are other rules to consider when assembling your portfolio. What irritates me more than anything else is the bad concept well-executed. This is a double negative for me because it betrays a lack of honesty and a lack of judgement on the part of the designer: you should never begin to execute a bad idea.

The idea is all-important and its worth should be scrutinised fully before going on to consider how it should be presented. So much design today is simply about surface presentation without content. At Minale Tattersfield we look at portfolios for evidence of drawing ability. But we want much more than glossy presentation skills: whatever the design discipline, we want to employ people who are skilful at drawing so that they can *communicate their ideas* and present their thoughts in a clear, precise way. We see drawing ability as a prerequisite of meaningful design, not meaningless visuals.

Another point to make concerns presenting your portfolio to a potential employer (a valuable forerunner to presenting it to a potential client as a design entrepreneur). Be confident, articulate and convincing, by all means. After all, design consultancy is all about telling the client to have the courage of your convictions. But don't overdo it. Some young designers actually have too much self-confidence. They are totally convinced that what they are doing is earth-shattering, that they are God's gift to the design profession. In fact they may have potential but they have a lot to learn and that unshakeable belief in themselves may lose them the job.

COMPLETING YOUR FIRST JOB

Having successfully targeted a design employer, put together a winning portfolio, negotiated an interview and landed a job, your first taste of life in a well-established consultancy will have put you on the first rung of the ladder to success at the head of your own design company. The problem is that there are rather a lot of steps to climb.

The first of these is completing your first professional job. It is a nerve-wracking affair. I remember that when I had finished my design training in Finland (quite logical for a hot-blooded son of Naples!) and had come to London, I got my first job as design director of advertising agency Young & Rubicam. In those days (the early 1960s) big design firms didn't exist and design was still largely subsumed as an activity within advertising. At Y&R I was set to work on day one on a corporate identity for Hawker-Siddeley. It is the worst job I ever did and, just my rotten luck, the company remained loyal to it for the next 20 years. When other firms were updating their identities, that Hawker-Siddeley image hung around to haunt me.

Symbol for Hawker Siddeley Ltd (Aviation and Engineering): 1962. Definitely one of the worst jobs I ever did. It still comes back to haunt me!

At Y&R I met my future design partner Brian Tattersfield. Immediately we understood each other. The first job we did together was a poster for Maxwell House coffee advertising three pence off. The convention at that time was to show the pack as large as possible, but we resolved to be creative within the constraints. Brian drew a slit in the top of the jar and showed three old pennies dropping in. It was a good visual idea which also followed all the rules. The account executive duly took Brian's proposal to the client and returned to announce that the client loved it. "By the way, just one thing," said the account executive casually. "Could you take the slot off, please?" 25 years after the event I still want to "kill" this account executive who had the audacity to "kill" such a perfect idea on one of our earliest jobs prior to Minale Tattersfield.

PLANNING FOR THE FUTURE

As your early days in the consultancy progress, your employer will be watching you for signs of development. Your chief priority at this stage should be to create a strong professional portfolio, just as you earlier developed a strong student one. You should also try to get some personal credit for your work, especially when it comes to public relations exposure in the design journals. That will, of course, depend on the policy of the particular design company. At Minale Tattersfield we have always credited young designers working on projects.

In my early days, the pinnacle of PR exposure was the *D&AD Annual*, chiefly because it was the only existing platform for innovative graphic design. Now there are so many design magazines on the market that a good piece of work will often have been published many times before it is seen in the *Annual*. This reduces the excitement, novelty and prestige of inclusion in D&AD and it is a shame. Nevertheless there are lots of different ways for young designers to make a name for themselves – and many do.

Over the years, between 30 and 40 designers have left Minale Tattersfield to set up their own design consultancies after working for us. It is a fact of life that if you give your designers contact with the client, most will eventually leave to try it out for themselves. But no more than 10 per cent of this number have been successful in the long term at running their own businesses. Those individuals who have made it share a number of common characteristics: they have remained true to their design skills, especially the ability to draw; they have been aware of the

A job done for 'glory' not money.
D&AD Annual and Poster 1981.

power of public relations to project themselves; and they have always been curious about the wider world and not cocooned in a designer ghetto.

In my experience, every designer whose prime aim in going into business was to make money while at the same time producing good design, failed on both counts. I believe that designing is something you have to do for love. If you are committed first and foremost to producing good design then you'll make money as a by-product because good design is something people are willing to pay for. But that financial reward will be a bonus, a gift.

Gaining relevant experience within a design company before going off on your own can be difficult to achieve because it is hard for an individual designer who begins essentially as a small cog in a large wheel to follow the *process* of a design project all the way through. I always say that the full gamut of experiences in designing includes making contact with the client, pitching for the business, winning the work, estimating the job, preparing the quote, creating the design, presenting it, revising it, re-presenting it, executing and implementing it, invoicing the client, disputing the invoice, re-invoicing the client, chasing payment, receiving the cheque four months later and banking it. How can a staff designer get involved at every stage in this way? The answer is you can't. But you can try to get as much of an overview as possible just by asking questions and looking over the shoulders of seniors. We all did it.

HANDING IN YOUR NOTICE

Once you have made the decision to go out on your own, then my best advice is to be totally straight with your employers. Tell them exactly what you plan to do. Most design consultants take it as a compliment to their training. They are also relieved that you are not leaving to join a direct rival and, provided you do not antagonise, they are likely to take a genuine interest in your welfare. Feel free to ask their advice because this is also usually appreciated. If you can't learn from your peers, then who can you learn from?

At Minale Tattersfield, staff have always been honest with us and we have always been honest with them. I cannot think of a single incident of unethical behaviour in 25 years in business. I believe that the paranoia that sometimes surrounds breakaway firms in the design business is quite unjustified. Minale Tattersfield did some research into the relationship between clients and professional consultants. We discovered to our amazement that, after doctors, lawyers and accountants, designers received the most loyalty from clients.

Companies tend to change designers only when one marketing director leaves and another joins, bringing his own personal choice of designer with him. The message of this research is clear: it is extremely difficult for young designers to "poach" clients and to break into the market, so mature consultants should have nothing to fear when employees leave to set up on their own.

The oft-quoted argument that the lower overheads of a design start-up offers the natural advantage of a cheaper service is also a fallacy. Design companies can't compete in the long run by being cheaper, they can only compete by being better. This is a lesson that many fledgeling design entrepreneurs only grasp through bitter experience.

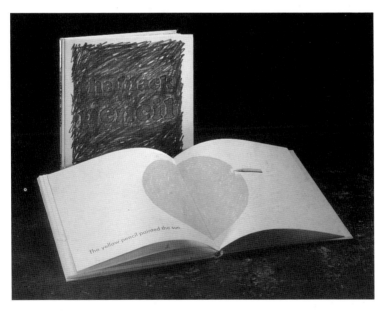

One of a series of children's books that I produced in the early days of our partnership: 1963. (Probably the predecessor of the Scribble.)

CHAPTER TWO

THE DEEP END – HOW TO START UP AND SURVIVE

THE DEEP END

HOW TO START UP AND SURVIVE

Congratulations! You've taken the plunge. You've made the big decision to go out on your own and start your own design company. There is immediately a feeling not unlike those characters in the classic old cartoons who walk right off the edge of the cliff and continue to walk on a carpet of air so long as they *don't look down.* The trick of surviving the first couple of years in design practice is not to look down. If you're the type of person who spends too long agonising about all the things that could go wrong, then you should never have made the decision to go it alone in the first place.

The beauty about launching a design business, of course, is that you don't need a massive influx of funds, equipment, space or stock. You can literally start up with next to nothing on a window sill. We did. In 1964 Brian Tattersfield and I established Minale Tattersfield in a tiny room on the Edgware Road in London. We didn't even have a desk. We produced all our designs on a window sill the width of an A4 sheet of paper. Not surprisingly, all our early work adhered rigidly to an A4 format.

However, the popular idea that you can start a design firm with no capital at all wasn't even true in the 1960s, let alone now. But compared to other industries, design has a very low financial barrier to entry. The first thing you should do, though, is find a good accountant who can advise you effectively on the mechanics of setting up your business. Even if you are planning a modest enterprise, my advice is to register as a limited company. This ploy will mean limited liability if things go awry, especially if you intend to buy print or other services on behalf of the

We started from an A4 sized window sill in the Edgware Road and arrived 25 years later at our present office in Richmond.

clients. It will also strike a more authoritative note with clients. Remember that, at the start, you are playing a game of bluff: you have to show that you are bigger and better and more experienced than you really are. Some design groups have in recent years taken this strategy to extremes by registering as PLCs through sleight of bookkeeping. But this is a confidence trick which can backfire, so beware. There is no harm, though, in simulating a certain business maturity at the outset.

CHOOSING THE RIGHT NAME

A key aspect of this is choosing an appropriate name for your design company and ensuring that your accountant registers it. But what name should you choose? Every designer wants to slap his or her own name on the door. It is part of the attraction of taking the plunge in the first place. J Walter Thompson did it. Young and Rubicam did it. So did Marcello Minale and Brian Tattersfield. The advantage is that you create an immediate and memorable sense of identity for your company as you meet clients in person. The disadvantage is that if there are four or five partners in the firm, you end up with a bewildering string of unpronounceable names and it becomes ridiculous. Practically half of the cartoons in the *New York Times* are to do with parodying the crazy names concocted by US advertising agencies or solicitors.

But if you then opt for a creative name drawn from the imagination, you can produce equally banal results. Designers are fond of describing the physical representation of their business. So we have Design Triangle or Pentagram. Or they try to sum up the nature of their profession. Names such as The Design Solution or Design Direction abound. Or they plump for intriguing, artistic-sounding titles like The Small Back Room or Joe's Basement.

The naming ideas keep flowing with every new design company which sets up, but on the grounds that the best abstract names have already been taken, my advice is to stick to your own surnames, especially if they are in any way unusual. I always thought that the unique combination of a Neapolitan name (Minale) and a Yorkshire one (Tattersfield) was odd enough to have some mileage in it. If you are successful over a period of time, the company name becomes a brand name and no longer an amalgamation of the surnames of the founders. I am sure that clients stopped asking for Mr Young or Mr Rubicam fairly quickly. Nowadays clients of Minale Tattersfield don't expect to see either Brian or myself at every client meeting. In fact some express surprise to learn that we're still alive!

PLANNING YOUR OFFICE SPACE

Young design entrepreneurs often make their biggest mistakes when setting up their first office. Two major misjudgements are to be found in this area, each one at the opposite extreme from the other. Many designers choose to work from home as a first option, or they decide on a lavish office with a prestigious central address. Both moves are disastrous to my mind.

The reasons why designers choose to work from home are twofold: first, they want to cut overheads, and, second, they want a greater quality of life through the idealistic concept of holistic living and working. It rarely works like that. As a designer, you must have a division between home and work. You need a pause in your life between the two: going downstairs in the morning, or even into the converted shed at the bottom of the garden, is not a sufficient pause. You need to walk, drive, cycle, catch a bus or train – anything so long as there is a division.

37 Sheen Road, Richmond. Today with modern communication technology and in-house services available at relatively low cost, it is not necessary for design companies to be in a central city location.

At the other end of the spectrum is the folly of spending money on smart premises with a prestigious central address. Remember two things: first, your clients won't be visiting you for at least the first two years – you will always be visiting them; and second, location patterns have changed dramatically in recent years. 25 years ago it was important when starting up in design to have an address in the centre of London or Paris or Milan. Now technology has rendered that necessity obsolete: the fax machine has changed the nature of communications while in-studio desktop publishing systems mean you no longer need to be next door to a district of typesetters and other graphic suppliers. Regional centres of design have sprung up in a number of countries, including Britain, which are away from the major capitals. Wherever you choose to open an office, you will always be conveniently placed for half of your clients and miles away from the other half.

The important principle is to avoid working from home or spending too much money on the design of your first studio. Once you have managed that then it doesn't matter where you go so long as you keep a firm grip on how long you spend there every day. When you start in business, the temptation is to work round the clock. But in my experience, the people who succeed in design are those who have the ability to switch off at around 6pm and not switch on again until the next day. The romantic notion of all nighters (a phenomenon exaggerated by living on top of your work) as an essential part of design creativity is a fallacy. If you are facing a series of all-nighters, glory not in artistic martyrdom but instead ask yourself why you are so badly organised.

It is a scientific fact that after eight hours of work, productivity dips and you are less likely to produce a creative solution. Stress is the kiss of death in design and overwork a symptom of stress. You can solve a problem in ten minutes if you are thinking properly about it. Spending 12 hours of distracted labour on it won't produce quality. Even the time spent on implementation has now been reduced, following the widespread introduction of computer-aided design techniques.

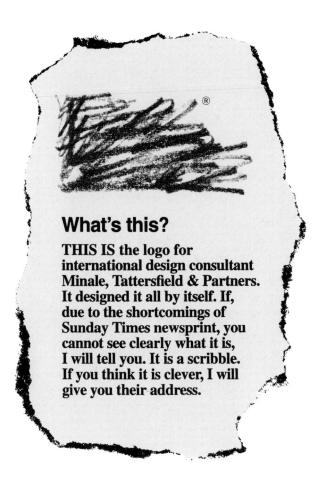

What's this?

THIS IS the logo for international design consultant Minale, Tattersfield & Partners. It designed it all by itself. If, due to the shortcomings of Sunday Times newsprint, you cannot see clearly what it is, I will tell you. It is a scribble. If you think it is clever, I will give you their address.

A nice mention in the Sunday Times 1965.

The primary tool of communication for any new design company is a well-designed range of stationery.

MAKING YOUR MARK

Once behind a desk (or leaning on a window sill) in your office, you will want to communicate with the outside world. The primary tool of communication for any new design company is its stationery. Many entrants to the design industry go in for lavish gimmicks, often expensively produced. I believe that you can impress clients and demonstrate your creative potential using single colour printing on a virgin sheet of white A4 paper. All you need is an idea.

In 1964 Minale Tattersfield made its mark as a newcomer with The Scribble, an identity which I believe remains as relevant today as it was then. The Scribble was created as a counterblast to the prevailing graphic convention of the time, when Swiss-Style dictated that all should be rigid, formal and symmetrical. The Scribble was ahead of its time and has done wonders for our company over the years. It has branded our design skills as witty, positive and emphatic, and it has been adapted and evolved as a graphic device, whatever context has arisen. Among its many incarnations, The Scribble has appeared as a crib on a Christmas card and as an army of worker ants for a self-promotional poster. And it reproduces on the fax like a dream.

Of course, an identity so conspicuously open to practical jokes has its downside. When we produced The Scribble on cheque-books, people thought we'd cancelled the cheque. I wrote once to the chairman of Iberia Airlines suggesting that we should redesign the company's identity; he replied that my letter was an insult, given that Minale Tattersfield had managed to produce such a dreadful solution for itself.

How would you like your agency to look like this?

At Minale Tattersfield we've designed many things for many people.

Things as big as the walkways at Heathrow Airport.

Things as small as our famous little logo.

Over the years, one of our favourite jobs, and one we think we've got better and better at, is designing offices for advertising agencies.

(It's not entirely surprising; Marcello and Brian did start life as agency art directors.)

Young & Rubicam, RMP, Kirkwoods and Lonsdales are four of our more celebrated customers.

As they will testify, we don't try to impose a standard, all-purpose system.

On the contrary, we start by asking everyone in the agency to tell us what he or she requires in the way of working space, equipment and furniture.

Then, and only then, do we go to work.

When we do, our proposals are always extremely personal, both to you and to ourselves.

The result: offices as individual as the agencies we

design them for. But with one thing in common; an uncompromising, single-minded attitude to standards of design and style.

If this sounds a little boastful you have a marvellous opportunity to judge our claims for yourself.

Right now, and until the end of the month, The Design Centre in The Haymarket has a major exhibition of our work. Please come along and take a close look.

If you can't make it, just call Marian Hawkins and she'll send you our regular newsletter.

Or, better still, arrange for Marcello Minale or Graham Simpson to give you a full presentation of our interior design work.

It's absolutely free.

And there's no obligation to buy.

But it may just convince you it's about time your offices looked as elegant as your logo.

Minale, Tattersfield & Partners Limited, Design Consultants, 209 Upper Richmond Road, Putney, London SW15. Telephone 01-788 8261. Telex 22397 Mintat Ldn.

By adapting our logo, 'The Scribble', we can communicate different messages.

THE WORKERS *Minale Tattersfield. Design Strategy*

Merry Christmas 1965

Merry Christmas 1990

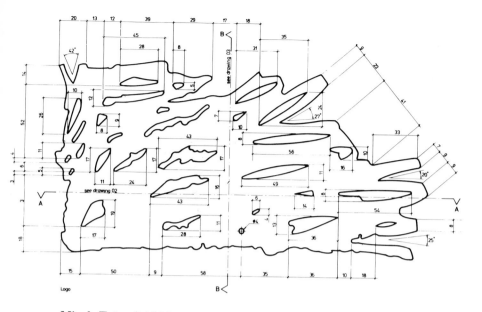

Minale Tattersfield Interior/Product/Environmental Design Portfolio

Minale Tattersfield Financial Design Portfolio

Nevertheless the inexpensively produced Scribble has worked for us. My advice in designing your own identity is to be brave, bold and ahead of your time. Too many designers regard the problem of their own image as insoluble so they opt out with a minimalist typographic solution which conveys nothing. Others try to look more like the client than the client. But the reason why clients come to designers is for creative ideas. So indicate your ability to think creatively on your own notepaper.

TARGETING YOUR CLIENTS

The logistics of naming and registering your company, setting up a studio and designing your stationery will occupy a great deal of professional energy, so much so that you can lose sight of the principal target: clients for your design service. Much has been written about how to target clients, but I would say that in this area at least, designers bear a strong similarity to insurance salesmen. Why? It is simple. Ask yourself: who are the first clients of the insurance salesman? His parents, his aunts and uncles, all their friends, the people he meets regularly in the local pub, the other members of his rowing or rugby team. Designers should start from exactly the same base. Your relatives and friends form your first pool of contacts.

The biggest mistake that you can make as a newly-established design consultant is to get hold of a copy of *The Times* 1,000 largest companies and write to the chairman of ICI and his peers telling them how great you are. It is a waste of 1,000 stamps. Your letters will be binned. You won't know the names of the right people to contact and once you have not got a reply from certain companies, it is extremely difficult to write a second letter to them.

I recently wrote a personal letter to the chairman of Swissair. I started: "It took me 25 years to write you this letter..." I got a reply immediately and he subsequently arranged to visit our office. If I had written to the chairman of Swissair 25 years ago, I would have got no reply. If I had written five years ago, I would have received a polite no thanks. But I waited until I had reached the stage in our design consultancy's maturity when I could be confident of a positive response.

We were lucky in our early years to get highly visible clients e.g. Harrods, Johnson & Johnson and the Italian State Tourist Office.

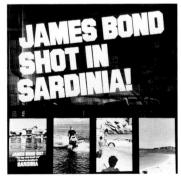

My message is that you have got to keep your powder dry and wait for the moment when you have got what the client needs. When you are just starting out, think small and target people within your shooting range. Later on, you can enlarge your aims. So don't go after the Swissair identity during your first fortnight in business. It is like stalking an elephant with a pea-shooter: you will only be a minor irritant.

After some years in business, you will find that it works the other way around. If you become a regular player in the international corporate identity market, it becomes difficult to go after a book jacket commission. But at the outset, the important principle is to be realistic and target your market carefully.

For the first three months there will be no cash flow, even if you are getting work and invoicing clients. So you need to fall back on savings, parents and a friendly bank manager. In the fourth month, cheques should be arriving but throughout your first year in business, you will have a period of grace. Even the most conservative bank manager will give you some leeway; friends and family will be spurring you on. Meanwhile, you will be on a permanent high, totally in love with your freedom, your creativity and your new enterprise. I always say that year one is the easiest year of a designer's professional life. It becomes much tougher in year two – when the honeymoon is over, everything catches up and you have to start making a living.

If you survive the second year without the financial and emotional crutches that invariably support the launch of any new company, then you are well on the way to succeeding in your venture. Throughout the second year, tensions and pressures will build up. But whether you are a graphic designer, architect or furniture maker, your priority should always be to produce interesting, unusual, creative design work. Once you abandon that principle and take on a job just because you need some cash flow and you think it will be a cash cow, then your venture will be in danger of crashing about your head. The safe financial options rarely turn out to be safe. The best approach is to press ahead with beliefs intact.

AVOIDING FINANCIAL BACKERS

In the same spirit of avoiding creative compromise, you should avoid financial backers like the plague. You do all the work; they sit back and take the money. I speak from experience on this matter. In 1965 Brian Tattersfield and I made the mistake of accepting £2,000 in return for giving away 33% of our company to a financial backer. We regretted the decision immediately and six months later we managed to get rid of our backer and reacquire our 33%. Since then nobody has ever backed us and we have never backed another designer, because we never wanted to be hated in the way we hated our financial backer.

My strong feelings on this issue can be summed up in one phrase: "Only a fool invests money in design." I firmly believe that design is not a profitable industry in the logical sense, with logical returns on investment. It is a vocational profession in which there are enough fools around to pay designers money for something they love doing. So my advice is that even when things get sticky in year two, don't succumb to the temptations of the financial backer.

THE PROS AND CONS OF A PARTNER

The question of whether or not to go into business with a partner is much more complicated. I am naturally an advocate of having a partner because I have survived and prospered in a partnership with Brian Tattersfield. But I recognise that it is by no means all plain sailing. There are pros and cons on both sides. Most of the other partnerships I have seen during my long relationship with Brian have collapsed, often acrimoniously. Brian and I even took on a third partner in 1966, an Italian by the name of Provinciali. It didn't work out. Three was a crowd. We went back to two, even though our poster advertisement read: "Two's a crowd, Three's a company".

The problem is that people change all the time. The person you go into partnership with at 25 will not be the same person at 35, 45 or 55. People tend to go in different directions and 90 per cent of all partnerships break up within the first ten years. Even longer-term partnerships are prone to collapse. Take Michael Wolff and Wally Olins. There are, of course, exceptions to the rule. Brian and I are lucky enough to be among the exceptions.

```
Min Alley Tattesfield
Means Ale Cattersfield
Mingle Tatler
```

One of the pitfalls of using partners names for the company title...

Our endurance is all the more remarkable in that both partners are designers. This is the hardest type of partnership to sustain. Design partnerships which match designer with businessman are usually better balanced. We have only survived because we have remained friends and we have continued to respect each other on creative issues. I believe that as soon as one partner thinks his colleague's design judgment is suspect then the partnership is as good as dead. There are no grounds for continuing to work together.

The advantages of having a partner are clear enough to me. Design has evolved in recent years so that it is less about the craft of the individual and more about the broad-based skill of the team. As a designer, your aim is to communicate, whether you are producing a poster, a chair or a hair-dryer. To communicate you need an audience. Your partner can act as this audience, giving valuable feedback at the conceptual stage. If two people understand a solution, not just one, then it has a better chance of being understood by the client and, more importantly, by the public.

A partner can also help to carry the load during the difficult early years of running a design practice, helping you to drown your sorrows, pick yourself up and keep on running. Even if you eventually fall out, then at least the partnership launched you into business and you can now go on and survive by yourself.

A perfect partnership – two people with different characteristics pedalling forward together.

Without a partner, you don't have the instant feedback and decision-making can be a lonely process. On the other hand you are your own master, you are in charge. You can take the company in any direction you want without justifying your action to anyone. I happen to believe that this can turn designers into megalomaniacs so that they eventually lose contact with reality, but it is clearly an attractive proposition for many people.

THE COLOUR OF MONEY

Whether or not you go into business with a partner, all your efforts will be in vain unless you set up a simple, efficient accounting and bookkeeping system to cost and invoice jobs. In a multi-disciplinary design company, this can become an art form in itself because there are at least three different types of remuneration involved. Each is based on a different principle and has a different timescale. Little wonder that multi-disciplinary design groups which floated on the Stock Market during the 1980s had such a torrid time: cash flow and profits are notoriously difficult to predict in design.

Graphic design income will be based on an hourly studio rate; product design income will be based on a royalty against production sales; and environmental design income will be based on a percentage of the total contract value of the project (similar to advertising agency fees based on a percentage of total media spend). Confused? Many heads of design consultancies have been. For now, though, all you need to do as a young designer is to follow some simple housekeeping rules.

Set an hourly studio rate which is not too low (as a guide, never sell design more cheaply than a plumber). When you start a job, give it a job number (always start from 100, the trick is to look longer-established than you really are) and keep an accurate record of hours worked on it. On invoicing the job, put the number of hours worked and the costs incurred, such as print bills, against the job number. Put a 50 per cent mark-up on your costs. So if, on Job 101, you worked 10 hours at an hourly rate of £50 an hour and incurred £50 in costs, you should invoice £500 plus £75, a total of £575. This is costing your company out for survival. But about half-a-dozen times a year the nature of the job – maybe the technical challenge or the tight deadline – will be enough to merit charging the client an extra design fee on top of your standard calculation of costs and hourly rate. This is the jam on the bread and it doesn't usually start happening until the second year in business. Knowing when you can charge the client that extra design fee is part of the intuitive skill of being a successful designer. Without it, you will only scrape by as a designer in business, surviving but not thriving.

Indeed the reason why so many designers face a bleak future in the 1990s is because they aren't prepared to put a premium fee on their work; instead they are prepared to give away work for nothing in speculative creative pitches. This trend is more dangerous for designers than playing Russian Roulette.

Designers should always know their worth, but sometimes money matters can have their funny side. I remember an episode in 1965 when Alan Fletcher, the graphic design guru, was asked to design a business card for the financial tycoon Bernard Cornfeld. It was one of Fletcher's earliest jobs and he eagerly received a phone call telling him to go to the VIP lounge at Heathrow to present the card to Cornfeld personally. He duly arrived at the airport to be told that Mr Cornfeld couldn't make it to London but would be in Geneva the following morning. Nonplussed, the next day, Fletcher flew to Geneva to be greeted with the news that Mr Cornfeld couldn't make it to Geneva but would be in Milan the following morning. Next stop for Fletcher was Milan where he finally presented the card to the jet-setting tycoon. On returning to London, Fletcher sent Cornfeld a bill for £1,035. Cornfeld immediately rang him from New York: "Jesus," said the tycoon, "that's an expensive business card." Alan Fletcher coolly replied: "The card cost £35. The rest was for the air flights and hotels."

CHAPTER THREE

IMAGE BUILDING – MAKING A NAME FOR YOURSELF

IMAGE BUILDING

MAKING A NAME FOR YOURSELF

John Paul Getty once said: "The meek shall inherit the earth, but not its mineral rights". I'd adapt that to "...but not the world of design". In my experience the successful design companies have been the extrovert ones which have not been backward at coming forward. Today the activity of image building through a vigorous and continuous public relations drive has assumed enormous importance in design: the 30-strong design group with 10 designers and 20 PR executives can't be far away. The act of telling others about your work has become more significant than actually doing it.

I would say that any newly-launched design company trading at a satisfactory level but looking to build momentum and gain recognition, should never overlook the value of PR. If you are producing successful design and having your achievements communicated to a wider audience via the medium of magazine coverage, then your fledgling venture will be endowed with a certain charisma and confidence.

But remember that PR is a double-edged sword. If you are having lousy work published in every magazine on the news-stand, then you will simply get a bad name very quickly. This is worse than having no name at all. The trick, of course, is to be discerning about what you release to the design media. Do not under any circumstances send the magazines everything you have produced. A lot of new firms make this mistake and pay for it.

I always make the comparison with playing soccer. Like design, you spend a lot of time passing the ball around, investigating and probing. Every so often there is a scoring opportunity and you make the most of it to score a goal. There don't need to be that many opportunities. A few exceptional goals can make a reputation and consolidate a career in soccer.

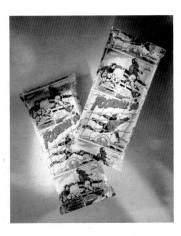

Football, Sammontana, Italy, Summer 1990. A few exceptional goals can make a reputation.

It is the same with design where, let's face it, there is a lot of grey, boring, competent, run-of-the-mill work being produced. But every so often the mediocrity is transcended by a flash of individual brilliance or a co-ordinated display of creative teamwork. These are the jobs to make a noise about in the press, just as TV coverage of soccer matches will celebrate the goals and forget the surrounding tedium.

As a design consultant you will want to be judged on your best performance, not on an average of all your performances. So try to build an image of your company around the handful of pearls you have produced rather than the inevitable abundance of pig's ears.

British Airports

*Two pearls—one for
BAA and one for
London Zoo.*

THE MECHANICS OF PRESS COVERAGE

Many designers look upon the workings of the media with a mixture of awe, fear and suspicion. They think that there must be some mystical, highly sophisticated procedure in order to make contact and that editors couldn't possibly be interested in what they have to offer anyway.

The truth is that it is a relatively simple matter to initiate a dialogue with the press, and in an age of media proliferation and ever-increasing competition, magazines are hungry for material. If you handle the mechanics of gaining press coverage properly, you can make the journalists do most of the work. But you should devote at least half a day a week to making sure you follow some simple ground rules.

Document your design work effectively. Invest in good photography to show it off to best effect. Write direct to the editor, or if it is a particularly large and busy paper, a senior journalist who has shown in previous coverage that he or she might be sympathetic to the style or content of your project. Present your work in a concise, professional way with a simple description of problem, brief, solution and outcome. Remember that journalists haven't got time to read accompanying thesis-length dissertations. Neither do they appreciate attempts by designers at "journalese"–they will want to write any editorial coverage in their own way.

Above all, a sense of timing is important in sending material to magazines and newspapers. Don't promote your new brand

OBSERVER

ESTABLISHED 1791   14 OCTOBER 1990   No 10383   60p

Way above average Underground

Architecture

Stephen Gardiner applauds the design for Hammersmith Tube station.

MINALE TATTERSFIELD are those brilliant designers of graphics and industrial products who are known not so much by name as by the excellence of certain things seen and used. Their delightful line drawings, for instance, of pyramids and other wonders of the world carry us along the travolators at Heathrow. Their highly imaginative posters put Milton Keynes on the map before a hole for it had been dug. The latest book on their work covers almost everything from a really smart look for BAA's Paddington-Heathrow express train to swivel chairs.

Now, however, they've moved in on another area, unheard of among graphic designers: they were appointed architects for the new Hammersmith station, at present being resurrected from the demolition of the island site next to the flyover, and across

the way from a collection of some of London's ugliest high-rise buildings.

Although the London Regional Transport Board is continuing to brush up the appearances of Underground stations in general, the Hammersmith scheme doesn't form part of the programme. In fact, the choice of Marcello Minale and Brian Tattersfield suggests that the board is making a special effort to recover something of the great reputation for design that London Transport had when under the direction of Frank Pick in the Twenties and Thirties. The board could have commissioned Elsom Pack and Roberts, the architects for the huge commercial development encircling both site and station, under construction at last after all the proposals turned down since 1979.

Now that both designs have been finalised, one can see why the board made its choice. While EPR's is a thoroughly run-of-the-mill affair, slightly tainted with the familiar overlay of Post-Modernism, Minale Tattersfield's has the sharp, telling imprint of a first-rate conception backed up by excellent detail.

The station has been devised as a simple element running through the middle of EPR's heavy development like a silver thread of very beautiful glass canopies and bridges, the composition and colour of which will make a fascinating centrepiece for those looking down from the surrounding offices. They're lucky: it's a pity outsiders won't have the benefit of such a view.

With the layout determined by external factors, it is the combination of an ingenious structure, economy of materials and clear colour that will accomplish aesthetic effects of great delicacy. In every case, the designers' ideas are sparked by interests of continuity — an awareness of the history of London Transport design, of the setting and locality of the station, and its closeness to the suspension bridge, the finest in London, over the river.

For example, there is an echo of the bridge in the station's structure: columns are dispensed with and the glass canopies over the platforms are suspended from five huge trusses.

Then the old frieze from the original building's façade has

been preserved, to be reproduced above the main hall in white lettering on a background of turquoise glazed tiles.

Below this there will be an enormous mural displaying the *reflection* of the suspension bridge carried out with glazed tiles in blues and greens on a white base, a typical example of Minale Tattersfield's decorative flair. These watery colours decide the theme for the entire scheme, surfacing in wall tiles, window frames and steelwork. Only the gutters to the canopies deviate: these use those of the Underground map — blue for the Piccadilly line, green for the District.

This neat device will remind passengers which line comes into which platform, and is one which might be employed throughout the Underground system in the colour of the trains themselves if they are ever resprayed. This would clarify directions in the maze of different routes in a graphic fashion. That, however, is by the way: the lesson this design so aptly demonstrates is that all the best ideas arise directly from practical solutions to problems, and their exploitation to an imaginative end.

Great white hope

P&G has given Daz Ultra a packaging facelift, designed to wash away its old-fashioned image and bring the new brand to prominence. Ken Gofton reports

She's a young, up-to-date housewife. A teenager in the 70s, she may well have a couple of children of her own by now. She knows what's going on in the world, she's aware of Green issues. And if she sometimes buys from the frumpier end of Next's offerings, that's just her touch of maternal conservatism.

Of course, that's the more positive side. Most people see her as hardworking and reliable, but sometimes a little old-fashioned and thrifty. She is both reliable and trustworthy, but a bit uninspiring.

Got the picture? Every brand manager has a mental image of his or her typical consumer, and this is how Procter & Gamble (P&G) sees the purchasers of Daz. It's the target audience Minale Tattersfield was told to aim for in redesigning the Daz Ultra pack which is just hitting the supermarket shelves.

Daz Ultra was launched a year ago – part of the stampede by the leading detergent manufacturers to market concentrated powders in smaller packs. And since design firm Minale Tattersfield was brought in by ad and packaging design manager John Fowler to develop a redesign as early as last summer, it has to be concluded that P&G did not get it right first time.

What we have, then, is a design dilemma. It's a dilemma, moreover, from the everyday, hands-on world of brand management, rather than the rarified world of creative awards.

Daz pack: last year's look

The detergent giant's first stab at the pack used design elements derived from the brand's earlier liveries, but the result was short on impact.

"I'd like to think that what we did was the design equivalent of the campaign for plain English," says Ian Grindle, Minale Tattersfield's creative director. "Let's use simple words where possible, let's use shorter sentences. For instance, the original Daz pack had stripes with airbrush shading. That's not a feature that implies cleanliness to us.

"We think our solution stands up better against Lever's Radion which is a crass bit of packaging, I don't know one designer who likes it."

The aim with Daz Ultra was to appeal both to existing and new users. Established customers were to see a brand name they trusted, but to be attracted by the "bright, colourful, exciting and contemporary design" to sample Ultra technology. Non-users were to have their preconceptions challenged by a pack which would stand out on shelf against its Lever and P&G competitors, such as Ariel, Persil and Radion.

"Ultra" may be a new variant, but Daz itself goes back to 1953 and in last year's Biggest Brands tables (May 24, 1990 issue) was the third largest selling clothes cleaning brand with sales of between £50m and £70m. Evolution is a familiar design problem: in an established brand, what are the recognition symbols, the core values, that must be retained? And what clouds the view, and can be safely disposed of, like murky effluent from a washing machine?

Daz was originally launched on the platform "Boils whites whitest of all!" The brand name – presumably derived from "dazzle" – was in white capital letters to emphasise the whiteness message, against a red background, with the supporting message reversed

Grindle..."we have changed every element, and yet it is still recognisable as Daz"

out of a blue panel. Much has happened since then. Daz has had "white strength", "new energy", "blue action", and "extra power". It has been able to cope with all kinds of temperatures, it has been "the AUTOMATIC choice for whiteness", and has offered "a whiteness that gets noticed".

The graphics have changed, too. Until the mid-60s, the brand name was in capital letters, and sloped down to the right. Then it switched into upper and lower case lettering, and started to slope up to the right. When Daz Automatic came out in 1978, the brand name was ringed by a chrome circle representing the front opening on a washing machine. This realistic symbol – still widely used by rival brands – has since evolved into abstract curves.

But there has been a lot of consistency, too. The core colours have always been red, white and blue – frequently supplemented with yellow. The brand name has always been in white lettering, usually with a shadow 3-D effect. It has been in "friendlier" upper and lower case lettering since the mid-60s.

And it has always been printed BIG. Such a short brand name means it can be printed very large on a pack face. And putting the word Daz on a slant, which has been the case for most of the brand's 38 years, allows it to appear even bigger. "We quickly found out what the key elements were," says Grindle. "Essentially, they were the bold, sloping,

sans serif lettering in white, out of a coloured background. The shadow was important, and so were the primary colours – it had always been a red box.

"If you analyse our solution, we have changed every element, and yet it is still recognisable as Daz.

"We thought, for instance, that the letter 'a' over the years had become ugly, and we redesigned it. The use of drop shadow under the lettering was very Superman, very comic book - but when you want to move something into the 90s, it isn't appropriate.

"Instead we proposed a double shadow that creates a unique Daz logo in place of just three letters. Having the sweep of the 'D' come in and out exploits the 3-D effect, but also makes Ultra an integral part of the logo.

"It's not one for the Design and Art Direction (D&AD) awards, but then P&G made it clear that it was interested in selling more washing powder, not winning prizes for creativity."

There is a postscript, which goes to show that even top designers don't always get their own way. In the favoured Minale Tattersfield solution, the stripe above the Daz D would have been a paler blue, like the stripe which carries the word Ultra: with packs stacked side by side, the effect would have been a blue wave running down the supermarket shelf. The word from P&G, though, was that stronger colouring was needed, so the wave was sacrificed.

Trade press: a nice article in Marketing magazine about our packaging design for Daz.

identity for a bottle of port in the height of summer. Don't submit ice-cream packaging in the depths of winter. If you are a furniture designer, try to promote your work around the time of the Milan Furniture Fair when there will probably be a better chance of gaining coverage for furniture-based projects.

Look for hooks in the national and international news which could make an editor look more favourably on the direction your work has taken or the clients for whom you have been working. For example, many designers have used healthy eating and environmental trends to obtain press coverage.

Your first target in the media should be the design press. By its nature it has a specialised professional focus, which makes it accessible to every designer who has something worth saying or showing. The design press is relatively easy to reach provided you observe a few simple rules. The national press is a far harder nut to crack. Here, you either need a long and successful track record or an element of luck. Tailoring your message to the priorities of the day or the mood of the moment can pay handsome dividends but it often takes a fluke for a design company to make the breakthrough.

The international press should also be targeted as so many clients today are multinational companies. Here, though, there can be problems of translation. I remember that my own company fell foul of this when we interested a Japanese publication in a story about our work on redesigning the bottle shape for Gilbey's Gin. A large banner headline announced:

International Design Press: Print Magazine, May/June 1990.

"Minale Tattersfield Expert In Gin Tasting". "Shaping" had become "tasting" in translation into Japanese and we were immediately branded as a bunch of alcoholics throughout the Pacific Rim!

ORGANISING THE PR FUNCTION

Given the importance of PR, many design firms look to PR consultants for guidance. But I would recommend that designers should handle their own public relations in-house and train their own PR manager. I have nothing against external PR consultants: it is simply a matter of culture and most outsiders gain little real understanding of the culture of a design consultancy, even if they are willing to learn.

Image building is such a delicate issue in making your design company successful that you can't let it out of your own hands. The old adage that "there's no such thing as bad publicity" doesn't apply to creative reputations. PR can be dangerous and it has to be controlled. An avalanche of the wrong type of publicity can damage a design firm or even an entire industry.

Take the example of the Memphis design movement in Italy. Before the launch of Memphis in 1981, Italian furniture was the world leader, popularly perceived as being beautiful and functional. The inflated hype and acres of publicity that surrounded Memphis – as every magazine in the world covered the new style with its crazy book shelves at 45 degree angles – turned Italian design upside down. It was no longer widely considered beautiful and functional, even if people liked it. And during the 1980s Spain and France successfully challenged Italian dominance in the furniture market.

Memphis' crazy shelves at 45 degree angles turned Italian design upside down.

The demise of Memphis and its detrimental effect on the classic longevity of Italian design demonstrates what happens when PR is wrongly handled and runs out of control. Designers in the past didn't have to worry about this aspect of running a practice. Publicity was never sought – talking about yourself just wasn't a very English thing to do.

Now media hype is an established phenomenon in design and it isn't going to go away. Its arrival dates to that period in the 1980s I describe as the *Oscurantismo* (or Dark Ages) of Design when the marketing men marched into the profession and told us that we must start marketing ourselves. PR is a prime tool of marketing.

Minale Tattersfield has not been immune to this influence. By necessity, we also have swum with the tide in seeking a larger audience and we have maintained a consistent PR programme. But as in other aspects, we have developed our own distinct approach in building our image.

We have always believed that image enhancement is all about giving people information. It is therefore a *cultural* activity and not a marketing activity. Our approach has been to achieve good PR by reverberation through exhibitions, publications and conferences rather than by making a crass head-on sales pitch. Our PR manager is our information manager.

If you simply inform people about your company in a dignified and entertaining way using a variety of media, then you don't have to prostrate yourself by cravenly chasing column inches. Minale Tattersfield's ambition was always to be a good design company, not a well known one. Once we had begun to deliver quality creative results, then a high profile followed. So many designers today want to be famous by jumping on a media bandwagon without designing the body of work necessary to give you that fame.

SPEAKING AT CONFERENCES

There is an important rule to observe in speaking at conferences to promote yourself. Only do it if you have genuinely got something intelligent and interesting to say. It is all a matter of timing. You have to wait for the right moment and the wait can sometimes be years. For instance, I wouldn't have sat down to write this book 20 years ago.

You can't just add water and – hey presto! – you have a successful design company. You have to develop your expertise and image drip by drip. For that reason I go against the grain of conventional wisdom, which says that you should try to get on as many platforms as possible to establish yourself early in your career. I think there is nothing more damaging than standing in front of your peers and bombarding them with an hour of self-serving nonsense. In 25 years, I have only made five conference appearances because I believe that it takes about five years to build up an interesting new professional perspective worth sharing with an audience.

When you don't know much about a profession, you tend to say a lot. Over the years you become expert and silent. I recently addressed a conference with the opening line: "20 years ago I had a lot to say. Now I've got nothing to say." In this context I make an analogy with rowing. I am a keen oarsman and coach. When I train young oarsmen, they say: "Why do you keep repeating the same things over and over again?" I believe that sport has a natural simplicity, like design. The message you put across is so simple that you inevitably end up repeating yourself. You can't alter the simplicity of the message, you can only complicate the message by obscuring it.

MAKING AN EXHIBITION OF YOURSELF

One of Minale Tattersfield's prime image-building vehicles has been a series of exhibitions about our work bridging commerce and culture in different world cities. Within the last 10 years we have staged exhibitions at the London Design Centre, the

MINALE TATTERSFIELD
AXIS GALLERY · TOKYO · 22-27 JULY 1988

Minale Tattersfield
'Veinte ãnos de revolución en diseño'

Our work has been the subject of many major exhibitions around the world: Above – London, Tokyo, Milan and Madrid.

En *México*

Minale, Tattersfield Designers
Museo Universitario del Chopo, Ciudad de México, Agosto 1992

The Scribble as a prickle on a cactus for our forthcoming exhibition in Mexico City 1992.

Padiglione D'Arte Contemporanea in Milan, the Centro Cultural de la Villa de Madrid, and the Axis Gallery in Tokyo. In 1992 our work will go on show at the Bienale in Mexico City. The exhibitions outside the UK have been staged in response to invitations from the city authorities. The authorities in turn were responding to information sent to them about Minale Tattersfield. The role of information in a broad cultural context should not be under-estimated: it can certainly help define, if not create, a design company's "profile". But your timing has to be right. You can't make your move too early in the development of your consultancy.

PRODUCING YOUR OWN BROCHURE

The production of an exhibition about your work is for consideration many years down the line. But the production of a brochure about your work should be a priority by your second year in business. You don't need a brochure when you first start up because you won't have much to say and you won't have done any real work on your own account. But by the time you have got a few successful projects under your belt, that changes and a brochure is an important image-building tool. The key questions are: what to put in it and how to present it?

There are many different ways to approach the problem. One method is to let your work speak for itself. So you just show large pictures of your designs with minimum description, perhaps only the name of the client. Today, however, the opposite tends to happen. Designers talk endlessly about the project without actually showing it properly: they produce reams of verbiage on the market, the client, the solution. Alongside all the analysing, philosophising and post-rationalising, the design is reproduced the size of a postage stamp.

This second pseudo-intellectual formula is a product of the rise of marketing and media in design. The market pundits and wordsmiths are justifying their role. However, it has caught on because the first approach relies on addressing a more educated client audience which can differentiate good design from bad. The second approach is more reassuring because its mission to explain in great detail makes both the designer and the prospective client think they understand exactly what is going on in the design process.

Perhaps the optimum editorial approach to the design consultancy brochure has yet to be realised. This is when you simply show the work, explain how much it cost to produce and use a simple mathematical calculation to say how much money the client has made from your design. This is the perfect brochure in a hypothetical world and it probably won't ever happen.

One of the problems of producing a brochure is that after six months it will be out of date as you develop new projects (although the design *content* should not be out of date after 20 years). The solution is to design some kind of container or folder which takes a series of single sheets. Each sheet should carry details of individual projects, so you can add to the publication as your business develops. The perfect-bound book preferred by some design firms is a waste of money in my opinion: it is there for eternity and your company will probably change next week.

Our brochure range comprises of simple unbound sheets. This allows us to have an up-to-date brochure that can be tailor made for each presentation.

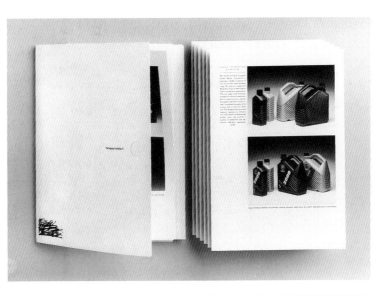

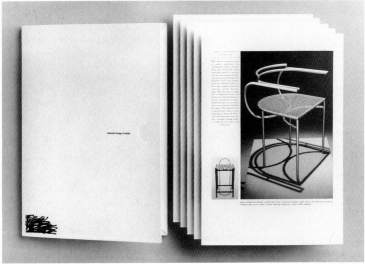

Depending on the format and method of attachment, your brochure comprising a series of single sheets can be flexible enough to enable you to tailor brochure presentations to individual clients. So when you write to a food manufacturer you can put all your food packaging projects at the front of the brochure. When you write to a high street bank you can leave out the work you did for HM Prisons. When you write to the Sports Council you can omit the furniture you designed for MacDonalds. And when you write to an oil company you can leave out the work you did for a Austrian wine company. Show the client what you think they'll want to see. Don't send every client the same statement.

COMMUNICATING WITH A NEWSLETTER

One way to keep in regular contact with existing and potential clients is via a newsletter. It is a great medium for communicating information. Minale Tattersfield started producing a newsletter in 1967. With startling originality we called it *The Newsletter*. It was produced on a shoestring and designed in the belief that people read personal letters. So it was designed on a single A4 sheet of paper and folded up to look like a letter. Because it also self-sealed, we even saved on the cost of envelopes. We sent out the newsletter once a month to about 200 people. Gradually momentum built up. In 1980 we introduced colour. Now our mailing list has more than 5,000 names. People as far afield as Papua New Guinea and Mexico learn about our work. Companies all over the world have written to us requesting to receive our newsletter.

Companies as far afield as Papua New Guinea have requested our newsletter.

In retrospect we were pioneers in this area. The idea has been widely copied by other designers. But our investment in time and money has paid off. One company in Brazil received our newsletter for 15 years before it contacted Minale Tattersfield to commission a major packaging project for the Brazilian market.

Recently we have expanded our newsletter, renaming it *The Scribble* to reflect a more mature stage in the consultancy's development. But we believe this latest format reflects the simple, direct, pioneering spirit of the early newsletters which did so much to establish our name.

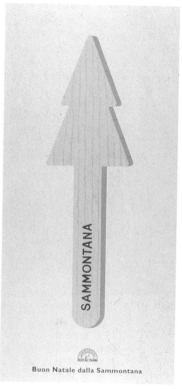

The Newsletter has matured with the company to become 'The Scribble',
which is now produced four times a year. One side always becomes a poster,
here it is the Christmas card for Italian ice-cream giants Sammontana.
(Winter 1990).

ATTRACTING THE RIGHT STAFF

If you inform people about your design company, rather than give them the hard sell, then you will gradually build a strong image which will have a number of positive benefits. Chief among these is the ability to attract the right designers. Consultancies are in competition for the brightest young talent, especially college leavers. If they have heard about you and admire your work, then you have a head start in recruiting them.

Minale Tattersfield has a policy of recruiting straight from college because we find it easier to train a new graduate rather than retrain a more experienced designer who may have learnt some bad habits elsewhere. We don't brainwash our graduates, rather we try to imbue them with a certain spirit. Above all, we have always tried to project the image of a centre of creative excellence in order to make leading young designers want to come to us.

You can see the talent-magnet process at work in other spheres. Why did Sweden of all places suddenly become a world leader in tennis? Björn Borg won several Wimbledon titles and Sweden's young players admired his exploits; out of admiration for Borg's achievements, an entire national programme in tennis gathered momentum. Why is Turin such a centre for car stylists? Giorgetto Giugiaro and his peers are based in the "European Detroit" and automotive designers from all over the world have flocked to work with the leading lights.

The trick is to inspire young designers and the right image will help you do that. But the power of PR and an assiduously cultivated image can only do so much to attract staff and win clients, *of course* people have to have heard about you. *But they also need to be sympathetic to what you do.* That is why the commitment to creative quality in design is so important and why the shallow pursuit of PR for its own sake can be a waste of time.

CHAPTER FOUR

THE PAY OFF – ATTRACTING AND RETAINING CLIENTS

THE PAY OFF

ATTRACTING AND RETAINING CLIENTS

The early panics and improvisations are over. You have established a foothold, you are expanding and you are looking to formalise your design business in a number of respects. So far, so good. At this point, however, it is not uncommon to become obsessed with clients. Where do they come from? Why do they come? What do they really want? Will they pay the bill?

A preoccupation with clients is only natural. After all, none of us would be in business without them. But you have to keep it in perspective. I don't believe in high pressure selling techniques so that you go chasing around after clients; such methods are often counter-productive. But I would be a liar if I told you to just sit back and wait for them to walk through the door. Clearly there has to be a balance.

If you phone up a client cold, you are in a far weaker position as a designer than if a client phones you following a recommendation. The nature and status of that first contact subsequently affects all future dealings, notably the type of work you produce. So the big question is how to attract clients and make them come to you.

AN INFORMATION NETWORK

I believe you can do this in a number of ways which fall under the general heading of disseminating information. The more methods you can devise to spread the message about yourself, the more clients will come to you. Over the years Minale Tattersfield has tried many ways to build momentum.

We noticed that the new generation of brand managers in companies was getting younger and younger. Therefore we devised an event at our studio entitled *Junior To Junior,* so that young brand managers could meet young designers of the same age to discuss branding and design issues. The event was a great success and forged many new links. In a similar vein, we organised a seminar in Milan called *Tutto Sul Packaging* to communicate our packaging skills to Italian companies. We used the image of an egg and a potato to explore the idea of beauty and function: both objects have the same colour and form but only the egg, in which you can perceive a "designed" structure, can be termed beautiful.

TUTTO SUL PACKAGING DESIGN, 23 OTTOBRE 1991, MILANO

JUNIOR TO JUNIOR

An Open Day for Tomorrow's Decision-makers
Saturday 24th November 1990, 11am to 3pm

Minale, Tattersfield & Partners Limited

Please remember to apply by 16th November
Contact: Liza Honey, Information Manager, Minale, Tattersfield & Partners, The Courtyard, 37 Sheen Road, Richmond, Surrey TW9 1AJ

Organising purpose-designed events and seminars is one
method of spreading information about yourself. Being seen
at exhibitions is another, especially if you are working in a
discipline such as furniture. Publishing should also be considered. Minale Tattersfield produced the first book about its work
within 10 years of starting up. That 1971 volume sold 1,000
copies. Subsequent books about our work in 1987 and 1990 sold
3,500 and 6,500 copies respectively. By tightly controlling the
design and production of our books, and by collaborating with
publishers who distribute and market the finished product, we
have never lost money on our publishing ventures. The value of
the goodwill and interest they create among buyers of design
services cannot be calculated.

*First book 1977
sold 1,000.*

*Second book 1985
sold 3,500.*

*Third book 1990
sold 6,500.*

Zanotta: one of the most prestigious Italian furniture makers became our client in 1967.

If the lateral moves of publishing books, appearing at exhibitions and organising seminars and other events appear to be part of a rather grand and aloof marketing strategy, then consider the alternative. You need a giant head-on marketing push to put your name about, as the large design firms of the 1980s realised. What happened then was that these firms began employing four marketing support staff for every designer. Overheads went through the roof, leading to losses, redundancies and much instability in the design industry.

Certainly it must be admitted that the multi-disciplinary design firm is the hardest to market. It takes a lot of patience and a lot of well-reasoned letters to the right people, pointing out relevant experience and any research you have undertaken pertinent to the potential client's problem. My advice is to just stick to one or two disciplines for the first few years – you can always expand your repertoire later. That happened with Minale Tattersfield. We began with graphic design augmented by furniture. Only later did we add other strings to our bow.

AVOIDING PIGEON-HOLES

If you are planning to build up a multi-disciplinary design firm, you will want to avoid being pigeon-holed by clients in the early phases of your career. It is they who hold the key to your future, no matter how much you think you control your own destiny. If all your early projects are in one narrow sector of the market, or for one high profile client, then you are likely to be branded as a specialist in that area.

Pigeon-holes are hard to shake off. Rodney Fitch's association
with retail design in the UK derives from his company's long
relationship with Burton. Michael Peters' image as a packaging
specialist is due to early work for such clients as Gauloises
cigarettes. Yet both fought to develop multi-disciplinary design
consultancies from a narrow base.

I can only say that Minale Tattersfield was not pigeon-holed in
the same way because of luck rather than judgement. No single
company or group of clients branded us in a particular direction.
But looking back, I recall that we only narrowly avoided being
pigeon-holed as television identity designers because at one
stage we were short-listed to create the identity for both Thames
TV and London Weekend Television.

Corporate identity for Thames TV 1967.

We pitched for both TV jobs, thinking we'd get one. We won both. At every subsequent meeting, the executives of one TV station would ask us whether we knew who was designing the identity for the other TV station. We played dumb. Eventually the crunch came. We presented the Thames solution first and this was approved. Then we unveiled the LWT design – appropriately enough at a meeting in a Soho strip club. We thought the LWT identity was even better than Thames and were confident of success. But LWT senior managers had learnt the dreadful truth, that we were also working for Thames, and our work was cancelled on the spot. So we lost a major job, but in retrospect we also lost a typecasting which would have been unhelpful in future years.

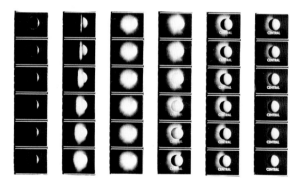

Corporate identity/signal for Central TV 1981.

THE CHANGING CLIENT

Of course, just as design consultants have become more sophisticated, so have clients. They are cannier and more demanding, and naturally I have mixed feelings about this development. Once they had a lot of respect for the consultant, standing back from the creative process and saying "you're the designer". Now they play a much more integral role.

I attribute this to the negative influence of the marketing men who marched into the design profession and convinced clients that they had a greater understanding of design and were entitled to exercise more influence. Consequently design has become like any other marketing exercise. Options must be explored and debated endlessly. The problem must be extended and dissected.

Instead of designers offering the client one optimum solution with maybe a couple of alternatives to provide some perspective on the preferred concept, we have reached the stage where designers bombard the client with a plethora of solutions at every stage – sometimes up to 70 different symbols on an identity project, for example – and the client picks the creative short list. This is professional madness on a par with being commissioned to write a magazine article and saying to the editor: "Here's the Oxford Dictionary, choose the words you like!"

I believe that as a designer you have a professional duty to stick your neck out. But it is becoming harder to do that in the current climate. Clients want to play their part and even I have

Various proposals presented for the corporate identity of Sawanoturu, the leading Japanese saké company. Sawanoturu means crane (bird) and marshland.

The selected one.
(Launched October 1991).

had to adjust my own mode of presentation in terms of problem-solving. Instead of offering the total, absolute, preferred solution, Minale Tattersfield now creates a number of options and allows room for debate. Our options are there, however, so that the white swan we want to be chosen will be noticed. In my experience the shrewd, bright client hardly ever makes the wrong choice.

There is a simple psychology behind this. I remember working in a Rome furniture store as a student. The shop was full of different models yet one settee sold all the time. I asked the manager why he didn't simply remove all the other furniture to make more room for the one popular piece. He explained that the settee wouldn't sell unless it was surrounded by others which made it look good. The customer could then make an evaluative choice. This is a basic lesson I have never forgotten.

NATIONAL CHARACTERISTICS IN CLIENTS

Different psychological approaches work in different countries. Clients differ dramatically depending on the culture and economics of each market. I'd say that the more common sense the client has, the more that originality and lateral thinking in design will be under threat. Logic is the enemy of creativity. Clients will find a way to talk themselves out of even the most intelligent and exciting solution. An excess of analysis can deaden the most vibrant concept. It is in this respect that clients have changed for the worst.

Nurtured by the marketing men, clients who are intellectually driven tend to worry about the problem so much that they won't ever see the solution. But there comes a point when all the discussion and negotiation must stop. After all, a group of people can always look at the outline of a cloud and some will see a monster while others will see a beautiful girl. North European clients, particularly in Germany and Britain, tend to be worst at debating *ad nauseam.*

Alessi lemon squeezer by Philippe Starck: A great job – only an Italian company could have produced it.

The Scandinavians, however, have a deep-rooted cultural respect for the designer which works to creative advantage and which is appreciated by professionals. Indeed the best clients are those which respect your professional judgement. Italian and Spanish clients earn my admiration because they act on the spur of the moment and don't stop to analyse. Their decisions are sensual, emotional and autocratic, and we can all see the brilliant results in the design markets of those countries. There is a much greater sense of discovery. I very much doubt that Alessi's enigmatic new lemon squeezer designed by Philippe Starck would ever have been made by a British or German manufacturer.

INTERPRETING THE BRIEF

Design without a brief is like a game without rules. If you try playing tennis without a court and without baselines, you become bored in five minutes: there is no meaning and no challenge. So it is with design. The brief defines the challenge. But as a young professional designer, you are also drawing up a set of rules within your own mind's eye – rules you will play with for the rest of your life.

So when you take on a design project, you have to obey both sets of rules – one determined by the client, the other dictated by your own head and heart. To extend the tennis analogy, your own creative conditioning means the rules are already fixed but the brief decides which racket and what tactics you will play with. Sometimes the two sets of rules will come into conflict. The client brief may request a trendy, flavour-of-the-month design with pastel squiggles; your own creative conscience will fight against such a solution. So the trick of interpreting the brief is to find common ground so that the solution satisfies both client imperatives and your own integrity as a designer. After all, you can question the client, even resign the client account, but you can't resign from your own deeply held professional beliefs.

The best briefs are those in which the client sums up what is needed in one sentence. You know you're in trouble when a thick document lands with a thud on your desk for a relatively small project. Distilling the information is a skill you learn through experience. Early in your career, there is a tendency to

Two posters. Top: for tennis tuition 1990. Bottom: an invitation to the Hangover Golfing Society 1989.

put a heavy emphasis on the wrong aspects of the brief. Later on, you know instinctively what to disregard and how to interpret the data so that complex phraseology is translated into simple, usable phrases. For instance, clients will resort to the most obscure and long-winded explanations to tell you something simple like "don't use black in Italy because it is the colour of death".

Subtext is important. Often the client really wants the polar opposite of what is written down in the brief. (This is actually not as strange as it sounds: the nearest thing to a design solution is its exact opposite). Often the brief is aspirational, glamourising context and object so that the designer is divorced from reality. Clients talk of making the housewife the queen of the kitchen when they want to redesign a brand of sink cleaner. I once got a brief which said: "We want something that looks like a Rolls Royce but drives like a Ferrari." The job was an industrial design for a heating firm.

Sometimes the mainspring for a design solution can come from what is left unsaid. One of the best briefs I ever received was in the form of a half-hour conversation with the client during which I did a spot of mind-reading. Nothing was written down. Indeed some jobs, a letterhead for instance, need scarcely more than a phone call. New rolling stock for a train, however, will demand volumes on the technical and economic parameters within which the designer must work. It all depends on the size of the project.

In whatever shape the brief arrives, the first job of the designer is to verify it by researching the market and collecting information to determine whether the objectives laid down are achievable. Often the brief will have to be reworked in part or whole so that it corresponds more accurately to reality.

Now there is a tendency for the client to overbrief the designer, to flood the design process with so much irrelevant information that creativity is paralysed. I always believe that you should read through these super-briefs, combing them for the pearls of wisdom that will act as triggers for the design solution. But once you have extracted the pearls, cast the rest aside.

THE RISK BUSINESS

Whatever you design for your clients, you are always spending *their* money. So there is a general rule which designers should apply to completed jobs: lock yourself in a room, close your eyes, imagine you have inherited a fortune overnight and ask yourself whether you would spend your own money on a design project executed in this way. If you doubt whether you'd spend your own money, then the client may well express similar doubts.

Design clients usually operate with a defensive psychology in what is essentially a risk business. They want to make their mark with their corporate superiors and often use the commissioning and management of successful design to get noticed. But they also worry about things going wrong. So there is a balance to be struck.

I have observed that the lower down the corporate ladder you go, the more adventurous the clients become. They are willing to take risks. If the design is successful, it will have a big impact on their career; if it fails, they will not suffer unduly on account of their low status. But the higher up the ladder you go, the more executives have got to lose. So they play safe and opt for conservative solutions.

There is a kind of inverse proportion in play. You can see it in the briefs handed out. Junior clients play up the glamour and are adventurous in their briefing. Senior managers tend to tone it right down. So the rule is: the lower the corporate ranking, the higher the expectation of the brief, and *vice versa.*

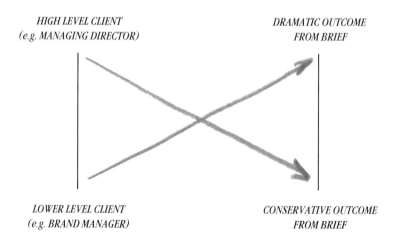

HIGH LEVEL CLIENT
(e.g. MANAGING DIRECTOR)

DRAMATIC OUTCOME
FROM BRIEF

LOWER LEVEL CLIENT
(e.g. BRAND MANAGER)

CONSERVATIVE OUTCOME
FROM BRIEF

*1985: clients logo in the most prominent position – right on the nose!
It was rejected.*

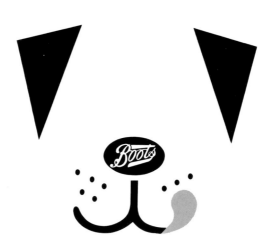

When staff at Boots briefed Minale Tattersfield to design new packaging for their cat and dog food lines, we were bound by a series of house style rules and regulations. We observed the letter of the law but not its spirit, placing the famous Boots lozenge logo in the centre of the pack and leaving it up to the client to decide whether or not they thought it was the animal's nose. Our solution was rejected. The senior managers who are guardians of the Boots identity deemed the design too radical – a decision which at the time verified my observation about seniority playing safe.

THE HEALTHIER HIERARCHY

Design consultants waste much time constructing elaborate management pyramids to establish links with the client. All kinds of client handlers, account executives and new business directors have emerged in the design business in recent years to facilitate the winning of work and the management of projects. But nothing I have seen has made me change my mind about one basic principle: clients should always have direct contact with the designer.

In a small graphic design firm, for example, direct communication between designer and client is the only way to maximise profitability. But even in a bigger company, the dealings should also be direct. Support staff should report to the designer who then deals with the client. When you have the designer communicating to the client via the support staff, then you can be guaranteed higher costs, poorer results and less profit at the end of the project, whatever the size of your

OBTAINING A JOB AND HANDLING THE PROJECT

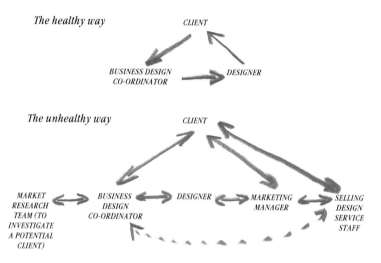

The healthy way

CLIENT

BUSINESS DESIGN
CO-ORDINATOR

DESIGNER

The unhealthy way

CLIENT

MARKET
RESEARCH
TEAM (TO
INVESTIGATE
A POTENTIAL
CLIENT)

BUSINESS
DESIGN
CO-ORDINATOR

DESIGNER

MARKETING
MANAGER

SELLING
DESIGN
SERVICE
STAFF

ORGANISATION FOR MAXIMUM PROFITABILITY

The healthy way   *The unhealthy way*

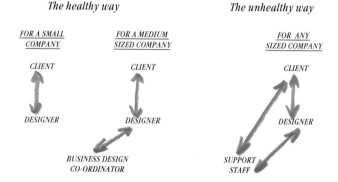

FOR A SMALL
COMPANY

CLIENT

DESIGNER

FOR A MEDIUM
SIZED COMPANY

CLIENT

DESIGNER

BUSINESS DESIGN
CO-ORDINATOR

FOR ANY
SIZED COMPANY

CLIENT

DESIGNER

SUPPORT
STAFF

For a small company – the client and designer, the only two parties involved, freely communicate with each other. This gives the greatest value for money and the best creative results.

For a medium sized company – the supporting staff reporting directly to the designer, who in turn deals with the client. This will yield maximum cost efficiency with good creative results.

This approach is unprofitable in that the supporting staff deals with both the designer and client. This leads to higher costs and poor final results therefore cutting any profit to a minimum.

company. If you are selling design services then you should make the designer the fulcrum and not allow market researchers, business coordinators, production managers or anyone else to lead the dialogue with the client.

PERILS OF PRESENTATION

But for all the principles of dealing with clients, and all the psychological tricks you can play, sometimes you are destined to lose whatever you do. More than ten years ago, Minale Tattersfield pitched for the interior refurbishment of Unilever House in London – an expensive and highly prestigious project – against another design firm. From the first meeting, we knew that the manager in charge of organising the selection of the design group had taken sides against us and favoured the opposition.

When we went into the final round with a presentation to the main Unilever board, I had the feeling we were just there to make up the numbers. How did I know? The rival design firm, Pentagram, made their presentation at 10am. We were scheduled to present at 2.30pm – after the board had enjoyed a heavy lunch. As soon as we started talking, the chairman fell into a deep sleep and punctuated our presentation with loud snores.

Afterwards we received a letter telling us that the chairman had been under great stress and that our presentation had not been jeopardised by his unequivocal response. I wasn't fooled. I had already prepared my reject fee invoice even before I got the rejection letter from the chairman. Looking back, I always say that the boss of Unilever made the final decision on the choice of designer – even if he did it subconsciously!

DECEMBER							JANUARY							FEBRUARY						
						1 2	MON	TUE	WED	THUR	FRI	SAT	SUN						1 2 3
3 4 5 6 7 8 9								1	2	3	4	5	6	4 5 6 7 8 9 10
10 11 12 13 14 15 16							7	8	9	10	11	12	13	11 12 13 14 15 16 17
17 18 19 20 21 22 23							14	15	16	17	18	19	20	18 19 20 21 22 23 24
24 25 26 27 28 29 30							21	22	23	24	25	26	27	25 26 27 28
31							28	29	30	31				

NatWest Calendar 1991: Leading up to 1992, the calendar linked common market member currencies to features of their national heritage or culture.

JUNE								JULY							AUGUST						
							MON	TUE	WED	THUR	FRI	SAT	SUN					1 2 3 4
3 4 5 6 7 8 9							1	2	3	4	5	6	7	5 6 7 8 9 10 11
10 11 12 13 14 15 16							8	9	10	11	12	13	14	12 13 14 15 16 17 18
17 18 19 20 21 22 23							15	16	17	18	19	20	21	19 20 21 22 23 24 25
24 25 26 27 28 29 30							22	23	24	25	26	27	28	26 27 28 29 30 31
							29	30	31					

SEPTEMBER								OCTOBER							NOVEMBER						
							MON	TUE	WED	THUR	FRI	SAT	SUN						1 2 3
2 3 4 5 6 7 8								1	2	3	4	5	6	4 5 6 7 8 9 10
9 10 11 12 13 14 15							7	8	9	10	11	12	13	11 12 13 14 15 16 17
16 17 18 19 20 21 22							14	15	16	17	18	19	20	18 19 20 21 22 23 24
23 24 25 26 27 28 29							21	22	23	24	25	26	27	25 26 27 28 29 30
30							28	29	30	31				

OCTOBER								NOVEMBER							DECEMBER						
	1 2 3 4 5 6						MON	TUE	WED	THUR	FRI	SAT	SUN						1
7 8 9 10 11 12 13											1	2	3	2 3 4 5 6 7 8
14 15 16 17 18 19 20							4	5	6	7	8	9	10	9 10 11 12 13 14 15
21 22 23 24 25 26 27							11	12	13	14	15	16	17	16 17 18 19 20 21 22
28 29 30 31							18	19	20	21	22	23	24	23 24 25 26 27 28 29
							25	26	27	28	29	30		30 31

NOVEMBER								DECEMBER							JANUARY						
					1 2 3		MON	TUE	WED	THUR	FRI	SAT	SUN			1 2 3 4 5
4 5 6 7 8 9 10													1	6 7 8 9 10 11 12
11 12 13 14 15 16 17							2	3	4	5	6	7	8	13 14 15 16 17 18 19
18 19 20 21 22 23 24							9	10	11	12	13	14	15	20 21 22 23 24 25 26
25 26 27 28 29 30							16	17	18	19	20	21	22	27 28 29 30 31
							23	24	25	26	27	28	29	
							30	31						

Two different solutions for two different museums. Imperial War Museum: Searchlights that form the initials 'WM' against a background of land, sea and sky denote war but do not glorify it.

Birmingham
Museums & Art Gallery

*Birmingham Museums and Art Gallery: The symbol had to unite
the different types of museum managed by the City of Birmingham.
The palette acts as a link between them.*

Two different corporate identities. Northern Foods: we tried to find the link between food and Northern and achieved it by using the Northern Star, which shines out at the top of the 'Plough'.

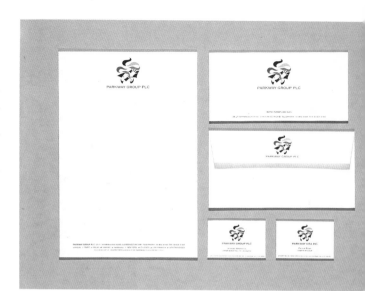

*Parkway Group:
The group operates
internationally,
colour services
being the
backbone of its
business.*

PARKWAY GROUP PLC

*The logo shows
a magician
pulling coloured
scarves from his
sleeve, summing
up the inspiration
Parkway can
add to a job.*

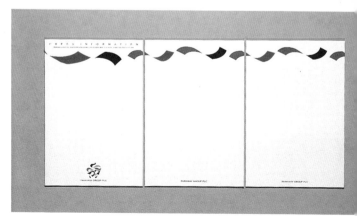

esting
to create
name for
napps,
ter than to
e Irish a
d drinking
und Haar
hair of the
atistics
at very
people
rman).

Sammontana Spa
increased their penetration
of the huge Italian ice cream
market from 6% to 13% after
a courageous policy change:
they decided to use top
international designs, namely
Minale Tattersfield, and
before us, Milton Glazer.

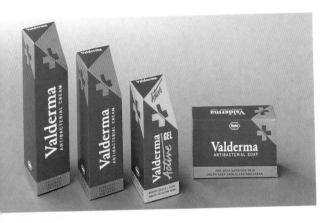

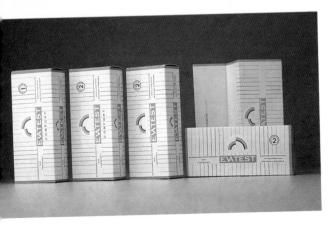

Valderma:
A brand where the
type of packaging
construction,
the cut-off corner,
creates the 'V'
of Valderma,
and consequently,
a unique presence
on the shelf.

Evatest: An
international
brand and a
difficult subject.
A broken rainbow
sums up the
expectations of
this test – whatever
the outcome
desired.

International packaging for BP oil now sold in 26 countries: a unique anti-glugging device in the neck makes pouring mess-free.

Future developments: experimental packaging for BP's synthetic oil using aluminium containers crafted to look like engine components.

Heathrow Express: A new rapid transit service linking Paddington station to Heathrow airport. The plan is to be operational by 1995. The wedge-shaped livery of the train echoes the romance of flying – on Concorde.

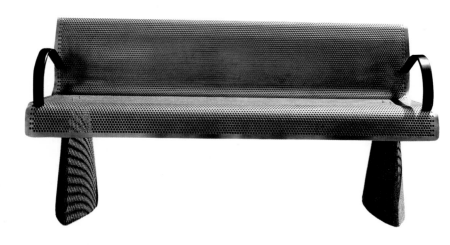

Steelgranite Bench Seat: A seating system for station concourses.
Truncated granite legs are ideal for 'clean sweep' maintenance.
Rising arms help the elderly in sitting down.

Hammersmith Underground Station: to be completed by 1993. An open air station on the London Underground system, its full suspended canopy will help to create an uncluttered platform. The colour scheme is related to Hammersmith Bridge, which spans the Thames nearby and the reflection also appears in the tiling of the main ticket hall.

DESIGN

Sunday
December 9

ROLLS
ROYCE
WEDNESDAY 7 NOV

BRITANNICO

TECNOLOGIA E INNOVAZIONE

MUSEO DELL'AUTOMOBILE–TORINO–DAL 7 NOVEMBRE AL 9 DICEMBRE 1990

*Design Britannico: A major exhibition of design and technology in Turin,
sponsored by the Foreign & Commonwealth Office. This was a classic
case of taking coals to Newcastle – i.e. taking design to the Italians.
The theme of the exhibition was based on the British weather and used
the essential elements of umbrellas and water.*

Closed umbrellas were used to display exhibit numbers and were suspended open to create a ceiling. Goldfish bowls were used for display, acting either as a stand or a cover to protect fragile exhibits.

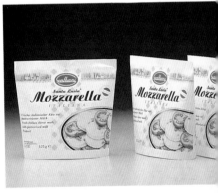

CHAPTER FIVE

DIVERSIFICATION – HOW TO MOVE INTO EUROPE

DIVERSIFICATION

HOW TO MOVE INTO EUROPE

You don't need to be a genius at psychology to realise that designers who establish successful and smooth-running companies are rarely content to leave it at that. Designers always want to seek out fresh challenges and explore new options: and you are likely to be no exception.

As soon as you have created a company that achieves a degree of stability, then you will immediately want to destabilise it by adding to it, changing it and leading it into fresh areas. Diversification is dangerously seductive to the ambitious designer who fears boredom, but it can often go before a fall in the design business. Consider my own experiences with diversification which are mixed to say the least.

Over the years Minale Tattersfield has diversified geographically, taking its design services into markets all over Europe and further afield. It has diversified in terms of discipline, moving from a base in graphic and furniture design to one which includes industrial and environmental design, interiors and architecture. Through an alliance with engineers and other specialists, it has diversified by combining design consultancy with engineering and product development consultancy in the transport sector. And it has diversified from a pure emphasis on design into manufacture, with a furniture company entitled Cubic Metre.

1975: Symbol for Cubic Metre furniture, a perfect solution to a simple problem.

DANGERS OUTSIDE DESIGN

The Cubic Metre experience lost us more than £250,000 in just three years. Looking back now, I realise how foolish we were to diversify outside design. So my message is simple. Diversify into new international markets by all means. Broaden your repertoire of design disciplines. Team up with engineers, architects or whoever in a consortium to give you a competitive edge in a particular sector. But don't step outside your role as a design company unless you want to go bankrupt and sacrifice all that you have painstakingly set up.

Not that Cubic Metre wasn't fun. It was. In 1983 we took a large shareholding in this furniture company and went on to produce designs and also handle all the marketing and promotional material. Of course we were arrogant enough to believe that we could do it differently, but in truth we should never have got mixed up in production.

We were always more concerned to produce outrageous designs than products that would sell. Even though we had become manufacturers, we couldn't change our behaviour as designers. We were always pushing ideas and conventions to the limit. Somehow we were never able to disassociate ourselves from our creativity to look at the consequences.

The main consequence, of course, was that we lost a lot of money. So we pulled out and let the professional people at Cubic Metre run it as a separate entity without the backing of Minale Tattersfield. The company survives to this day. The experience taught us a valuable lesson that all our subsequent diversification should retain the design consultancy at its core.

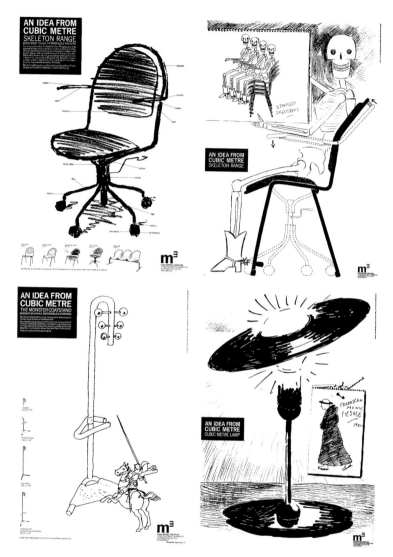

Having designed the furniture for Cubic Metre, Brian Tattersfield had great fun designing these promotional posters.

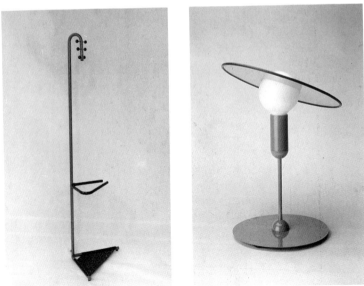

Skeleton range, Monster coatstand and Fiesole lamp.

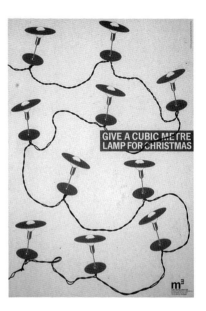

GIVE A CUBIC METRE
LAMP FOR CHRISTMAS

CHRISTMAS GREETINGS FROM CUBIC METRE FURNITURE

Cubic Metre Christmas cards: the three 'm's as camels, Christmas lights and Joseph the carpenter.

ALLIANCE WITH ENGINEERS

In diversifying to create a multi-disciplinary team, I have found that the addition of architectural, interior and industrial design to our graphic and furniture expertise has had a profound cultural influence on the consultancy over the years. But such is the sophistication of certain specialist market sectors today that even a broad spectrum of skills within a design company is no guarantee of success.

Clients are increasingly demanding a "turnkey" service in which products and systems are not just designed but also proto-typed, tested, engineered and built. Nowhere is this more apparent than in the transport sector, an acknowledged growth area for multi-disciplinary design and engineering skills. So Minale Tattersfield has formed a consortium entitled Transpartners in which our particular expertise is teamed with three other companies – engineering practice Mott MacDonald, vehicle development and prototyping company MGA, and rail transport designers Trevor Scott Associates – to provide a fully integrated approach.

Logo for the new Transport Design consortium founded in 1991.

This is one example of diversification in which our horizons have been broadened without moving away from the core services in design consultancy which our company provides.

THE CHALLENGE OF EUROPE

Transpartners was conceived to operate on an international basis, just as Minale Tattersfield itself is active in international markets. But the creation of such a broad canvas for our work has not been achieved overnight. On the contrary, our status as an international design consultancy has taken 15 years to build up. So if you are considering diversifying overseas, then you should be prepared for a long, hard slog.

The first destination for any British design firm seeking to expand internationally is invariably continental Europe. The reasons are obvious: the design markets of Europe are close at hand and do not necessitate exhausting long haul flights (it can sometimes be easier to get to Brussels in the morning than Birmingham); they admire many aspects of British design; and they provide a welcome escape for designers from the constant traumas of the UK economy and the antipathy towards design in many sections of British industry.

But the big question is always which European markets you should attempt to enter first. In the case of Minale Tattersfield, it was Holland and Germany – two of the most sophisticated design markets in Europe at the time (the early 1970s). The level of acceptance of our packaging and corporate identity work confirmed my belief that you should never try to sell your design services into markets which aren't sophisticated or mature enough to understanding what it is you are offering.

It is entirely fallacious to suggest that just because a country has no indigenous design market or activity, there will automatically be a market for your consultancy's work. The likelihood is that your work will be ignored or misunderstood. Either way it won't be accepted. I make an analogy with taking Shakespeare around the world: his plays have a far greater chance of being appreciated in countries with a literary tradition where people can actually read. So it is with design where a visual tradition and some awareness of good design must be part of the culture before you can hope to succeed.

FIRST STEPS ABROAD

I well remember our first tentative steps overseas. Lever Holland asked us to redesign the packaging for Persil for the Dutch market. So in 1973 we jumped on a plane and were met at Schipol Airport, Amsterdam, by Persil's marketing manager. He took us to his car and Brian and I sat meekly in the back while he drove us to our meeting. Throughout the journey he kept breaking hard for no good reason. His behaviour was alarming. We reached his office in a state of shock. His driving had reduced us to a pair of gibbering wrecks. Was this the psychology of the foreign client? We asked ourselves if his intention was to shake us up and disorientate us totally. It was a curious first contact with a continental commission.

The story took an even worse turn when I returned to Amsterdam to present our design solution. I developed a bad back on the flight and had to be lifted from the plane and taken to the presentation in a wheelchair. I then delivered the presentation standing up because it was too painful to sit down. Despite all this, we still managed to successfully complete the job and begin what has turned out to be a long relationship with the Dutch market.

Other commissions followed from Dutch airline companies, including KLM. Then the German market beckoned with a commission from Henkel to repackage its Dixan washing powder, and Swiss chocolate maker Suchard also gave us work. Our strategy at this time was simple: get on a plane to get the brief, and do all the creative work back in London. Our selling point was that we offered a different point of view and a different way of doing things. Even at this early stage we resolved that under no circumstances would we open a design office in any country without having first built a market there.

By the time we were asked by Imperial Tobacco to work on a mild cigarette called Gladstone for the Dutch market, we were almost old hands at the game. Unfortunately I chose to relax too much. One cold winter's day I spent about five hours art directing a moody shot on a Dutch beach. Throughout the session I kept sipping from a bottle of brandy to ward off the freezing conditions. Immediately the shoot was over, I made a long car journey to see the client. Infused with alcohol, I fell asleep in the back of the car with the heater on. By the time I reached the meeting I was totally paralytic. I could barely stand up. I had to apologise for the state I was in. The Dutch took it well. They understand about these things.

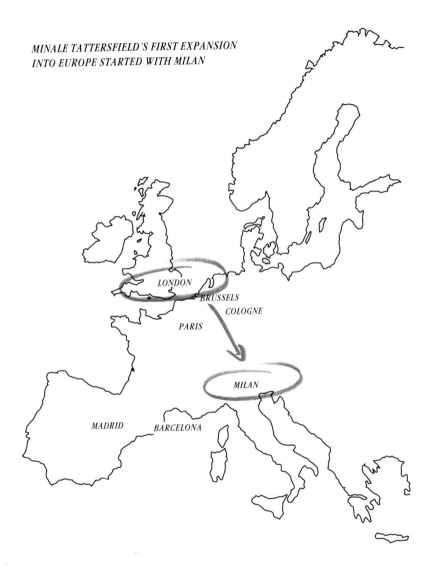

MINALE TATTERSFIELD'S FIRST EXPANSION
INTO EUROPE STARTED WITH MILAN

LONDON

BRUSSELS

COLOGNE

PARIS

MILAN

MADRID   BARCELONA

THE ITALIAN CONNECTION

Naturally, having "cleaned up" in Northern European with various washing powder pack designs, Minale Tattersfield looked south to Italy where I have strong personal and cultural connections. Our work in Italy began in the 1970s with various posters, promotions and window displays for such clients as the Italian Institute for Trade and the Italian State Tourist Office. But by the 1980s we wanted to raise our profile in the Italian market in a more significant way. We also resolved to go directly to clients for commissions, rather than work for them indirectly via advertising agencies – as in Holland and Germany.

That called for a new strategy to change the pattern of obtaining work and make a more direct appeal to companies. We could have written 10,000 letters to senior Italian industrialists. But we knew that would have stood little or no chance of success. So instead we staged our first major overseas exhibition, relying on the medium of information and culture to market our name in Italy. In 1981 we had staged an exhibition of our work at the Design Centre in London. On the strength of that we were invited in 1983 to exhibit at the Padiglione D'Arte Contemporanea in Milan by the city authorities.

The show was visited by an estimated 30,000 people and was very well-received. It opened many eyes to the idea of graphic design as a commercial activity in a market which had previously envisaged it only as art. Following the exhibition, a nucleus of about 20 major Italian clients approached us to collaborate with them. The strategy had worked. As I have

MARCELLO
MINALE

BRIAN
TATTERSFIELD

Minale, Tattersfield & Partners (Packaging Design and Corporate Identity) Head Office: Burston House, Burston Road, Putney, London SW15 6AR Telephone: 01-788 8261 Telex: 22397 Mintat G

Rappresentanza per l'Italia: Minale, Tattersfield & Partners, Via Petrarca 4, 20123 Milano Tel: 498 3514/498 5483 Contatto: Ida Morazzoni o Toti Melzi D'Eril

The introduction of Ida Morazzoni and Toti Melzi D'Eril at our Milan office in 1980 called for this poster.

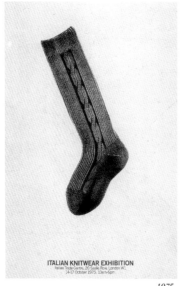

ITALIAN KNITWEAR EXHIBITION
Italian Trade Centre, 20 Savile Row, London W1,
14-17 October 1975, 10am-6pm.

ITALIAN CHILDREN'S WEAR EXHIBITION
Italian Trade Centre, 20 Savile Row, London W1,
19-22 March 1979, 11am-7.30pm

1975

1979

1978

*Italian State Tourist Office and the Italian Trade Centre were
a gift for our creativity in the 1970s.*

1983: catalogue for our exhibition in Milan.

said before, you are always in a much stronger position to sell a radical solution for a premium price if the client comes to you than if you chase after the client.

Fashion guru Giorgio Armani, top ice cream maker Sammontana, mineral water giant San Pellegrino and leading furniture company Zanotta were just some of the names to join our client list. Our links with Italy have been strengthened since. In a further act of diversification, we set up the Financial Design Company in association with an Italian design firm in March 1989 in order to service the growing market in financial services literature.

*1984: ice cream for Sammontana. 1989: 100% Juice packaging for
San Pellegrino.*

FINANCIAL DESIGN C<u>O</u>

DECIMO ANNIVERSARIO
1980 - 1990

SO.PA.F.

Top: packaging for Armani underwear with a completely new construction.
Middle: 'F' of the Financial Design company shown as a bar graph.
Bottom: 10% of a pie-chart represents the 10th Anniversary of SO.PAF.

SPANISH STEPS

We repeated the pattern in more or less the same way in Spain to present our credentials in what proved to be one of the most exciting design markets of the 1980s. In 1985 we were invited to exhibit at the Centro Cultural de la Villa in Madrid. The show, again bridging the gulf between commerce and culture, attracted similar numbers to the Italian exhibition and equally warm reviews. Spanish newspaper *El Pais* was as enthusiastic as Italy's *La Republicca* had been.

The exhibition format, later reinforced by the publication of the *Design A La Minale Tattersfield* book in 1985, set the pattern for our expansion in Europe and beyond. We subsequently staged an exhibition at the Axis Gallery in Tokyo in 1987 as a prelude to our entry into the Japanese market and, as I write, we are preparing to exhibit in Mexico City in 1992.

Minale Tattersfield
'Veinte ãnos de revolución en diseño'

1985: poster for our exhibition in Madrid.

The point about producing exhibitions and books as tools to inform people, rather than marketing your design company in a conventional way, is that you must get it right. You need to stimulate and excite. If you produce a book full of rubbish or a boring exhibition, then you will only alienate your potential audience.

In Spain we made what appeared to be the right moves, winning work in retailing for Galerias Preciados and in broadcasting for independent TV station Antenna 3. But such is Spain's importance in the run-up to 1992 with the Seville World Expo and the Barcelona Olympics that we decided to seek a collaboration with a local partner to strengthen our position in the market. Our research led us to Carlos Rolando, one of Europe's leading graphic designers, who had created the Seville Expo'92 identity. Only after we had signed the deal uniting our companies in Spain, he reminded us that he'd applied to Minale Tattersfield in 1965 for a job. We had turned him down! Our rejection clearly hadn't prevented him from prospering on the international stage.

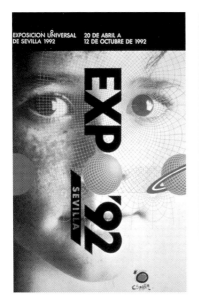

Great jobs for Barcelona Olympics and Expo '92 by our Spanish partner Carlos Rolando.

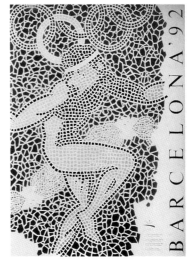

A STRATEGY FOR FRANCE

Our approach to the French market needed to differ from the Italian and Spanish models. A cultural soft sell via the medium of an exhibition was not considered likely to succeed given the tradition of French insularity and national chauvinism. The French stand very much aloof from the mainstream of European design and the market is one of the toughest to crack, as many UK design firms have discovered to their cost. We decided that the only way forward in France was to find a French partner.

We knew of Design Strategy, the French market leader in corporate identity, and approached its partners with a view to a merger between the two companies. After discussions with Belgian Philippe Rasquinet and American Jim Waters of Design Strategy, we formed an alliance in autumn 1989 to create a new Anglo-French axis in international design. Minale Tattersfield Design Strategy, as the group is now known, has a strong presence in Europe which has paid off for us. Take, for example, the body of work associated with the Channel Tunnel link. Minale Tattersfield pitched for the corporate identity of the Channel Tunnel Eurostar train and lost, but Design Strategy did the same and won. So even though we lost, we won.

EXCHANGING EQUITY

I wouldn't like people to get the wrong idea, though, about the nature of our mergers and alliances in Europe. These aren't big business machinations. No money changes hands. The deals with

Packaging for Gini, corporate identity for BNP and logo for UAP Assurance by our French partners Philippe Rasquinet and Jim Waters at Design Strategy.

Design Strategy and Carlos Rolando are based on an exchange of equity only. Our firm principle has always been to avoid acquiring companies with money.

The oldest truism in the book is that design is a "people business" and people tend to walk out of the door. You can't buy loyalty for cash. It has been proved again and again that once the principals of acquired design companies have completed their earn-out contracts, they leave behind little more than a shell no matter how much they originally sold out for.

My advice is that equity swaps should be staged progressively to bring design companies together. Start with a small exchange and increase the percentage if all goes well. Full-blown acquisitions are unhealthy. They don't work and they create ill feeling. Personally, I'd never invest a penny of my own money in design. It is a great area to be involved in professionally, but it is not an area for investment. It is far better to find a group of like-minded designers for whom you have creative respect and reach an agreement to share equity in each other's companies. It beats marching in behind a posse of lawyers wielding a cheque book.

In the case of Jim Waters and Philippe Rasquinet of Design Strategy, both had worked in the UK design market and we respected what they did. You need the basis of respect to expand via a series of alliances in Europe. I'd contend that conventional business deals don't really work in the design context.

EUROPE'S BEST CLIENTS

Our tie-up in France with Design Strategy led us into Belgium. Our experiences in Italy and Spain prepared us for work in Greece. The Minale Tattersfield name is now visible throughout northern and southern Europe. But there is no doubt that I prefer the Latin clients – the Italians, Spaniards and Greeks – because they respect the creativity of the designer. The Germans, by contrast, simply use the designer as a marketing tool to test facts.

I remember one German client who told us that the front of our pack had researched well but not the back and sides. So we modified our design. They came back to us and said that the research feedback was that the sides and back were good but not the front. So we made a further change. This time the feedback was that the front and sides were fine but not the back. This went on and on. In truth we design for the totality. To research a piece of packaging in such a way is ludicrous.

The Germans are often too intellectually driven in design. They rely on research rather than their own creative convictions. It is worth remembering that leading German designer Richard Sapper didn't design the famous Tizio light until he lived in Milan where Italian sensuality could soften Teutonic engineering.

When Minale Tattersfield produced a flyer promoting our international client list, we cheekily compared different clients to make a series of jokes, for example London Transport with a can of Harrods sardines. The Germans were destined to come in for some rough treatment given how we had suffered at their hands over the years: we juxtaposed the German Wine Association with a can of BP anti-freeze!

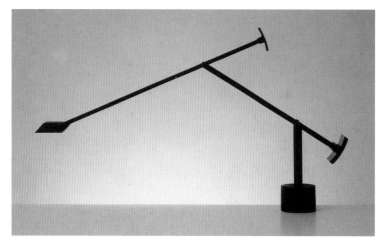

Tizio lamp – one of the great modern classics by Richard Sapper.

The British suffer from many of the same hang-ups as the Germans. If you can compare the British and Italian furniture industries, they are polar opposites. While British furniture companies try to read the mind of the public by carrying out market research into what they want to buy, the Italians are much more liberated in their thinking: they will produce lots of original ideas, put on show maybe 40 prototypes, and let the market decide which ones should go into production.

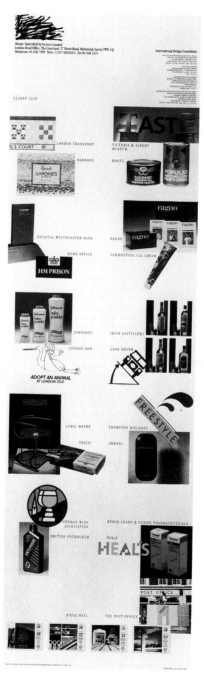

Client list – pairing clients through a common denominator, like Harrods sardines compared to the London Underground. See if you can find out the rest for yourself.

BRITISHNESS IN DESIGN

I believe there is a role, however, for a distinctive British identity in design. It is clear to me that those British products which have achieved success in world markets are those which have retained an essence of Britishness, rather than those which have consciously aimed for global acceptance. If you take the automotive sector, Jaguar and Range Rover are good examples. UK attempts at a world car have failed.

In November 1990 Minale Tattersfield designed an exhibition for the Foreign Office in Turin entitled *Design Britannico*. The British design on show ranged from Rolls Royce engines to Tube posters. In preparing the exhibition – which incidentally featured such design details as umbrellas suspended upside down from the ceiling and nautical elements suggesting the UK's naval history – I began to think about the characteristics of British design in the context of Europe and the world market.

It occurs to me that for most of this century the world has looked to America for lessons in how to *consume*. Now the world could well start looking to Europe for lessons in how to *conserve*. And who better than the British – producers of sensible shoes, quality raincoats, and other classic, long-serving merchandise – to lead the way out of our throwaway culture. The real winners in tomorrow's markets will be those who produce and consume less, not more.

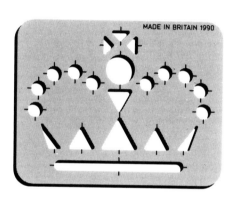

MADE IN BRITAIN 1990

DESIGN BRITANNICO
TECNOLOGIA E INNOVAZIONE

MUSEO DELL'AUTOMOBILE - TORINO
7 NOVEMBRE - 8 DICEMBRE 1990

Souvenir poster commemorating an exhibition of British design.

Minale Tattersfield
Design Strategy

TAKING EUROPEAN DESIGN
TO THE WORLD

LONDON · PARIS · MILAN · MADRID · COLOGNE · CASABLANCA · NEW YORK

HONG KONG · OSAKA · BRISBANE · SYDNEY

SOME OF OUR CLIENTS

GREAT BRITAIN
BP Oil International
British Airports Authority
British Rail
Cable & Wireless
Central TV
Charter Group
Foreign Commonwealth Office
Harrods
Heathrow Express
House of Fraser
Imperial War Museum
International Distillers
& Vinters
James Burrough Distillers
London Transport
National Westminster Bank
Northern Foods
Natural Resources Institute
Parkway
Port of Dover
Princeton
Warerite

FRANCE
Banque de France
Banque Hervet
Banque Indosuez
BNP
Bull
Centrale de Banques
France Telecom
General Foods
Grands Moulins de Paris
Group Suez
Kodak
L'Oréal
Martini
Memorex
Ministère des Finances
Peugeot
Renault
Rhône · Poulenc
Spontex
Transmanche
Union de Banques à Paris
Waterman

ITALY
Boehringer
Coin
Fendi
Ferrero
Giorgio Armani
Gucci
Mantero
Max Meyer
Misura
Nestlè
Parkway
Ragno
'Sammontana

San Pellegrino
Soilax
Valentino

SPAIN
Galerias Preciados
Antenna 3 Station TV

BELGIUM
Assurances Générales
ANHYP
Banque Nagelmackers
De Beers

FINLAND
Oy Stockman

IRELAND
Irish Distillers
Belfast Wine Warehouse
Dale Farm

GERMANY
Boehringer
Ferrero
Henkel
Reemtsma
Optyl

SWITZERLAND
Firmenich
Nestlè
Suchard

NETHERLANDS
Heineken
Imperial Tobacco
Unilever
DMV Campina

CARIBBEAN
Cable & Wireless

BRAZIL
Kiviks Marknad

AUSTRALIA
Hotels Hyatt
Expo Exhibition Queensland
National Sports Centre
National Trust Australia
Brisbane International Airport
Brisbane City Council

JAPAN
Fuji
Kansai Paint
Lilac
Toyota

HONG KONG
Cable & Wireless
The Garden Company

If you'd like more information or you would like a copy of
the quarterly newsletter "The Scribble" please contact
the Information Department, Minale Tattersfield and Partners,
The Courtyard, 37 Sheen Road, Richmond, Surrey TW9 1AJ Fax (01) 948 2435

An advertisement of our sales strategy: selling European design to the world.

TAKING EUROPE TO THE WORLD

Indeed the focal concept of European design as a covetable symbol of quality and up-market aspiration around the world is looking increasingly attractive to me. It has worked for leading European fashion and cosmetics houses such as Armani, Chanel and Valentino, who have sold the European idea of style and dressing globally, and it has certainly inspired Minale Tattersfield's slogan, "Taking European Design To The World."

OLI(V)IEW ®

We always insist that we are "European designers". To us, international business means an Italian client asking us to design a brand for the Japanese market. Just because we work internationally doesn't mean we design in a bland global-marketing style. Our interpretation of a product or identity is always from a European standpoint wherever the client is based in the world.

From Perrier to Alessi, European design reflects the idea of quality production whereas American design symbolises mass production. The Alfa Romeo Spider, for example, is a car that could never have been produced by General Motors. That is why I am so confident about the future of European design. We are fast entering a world in which the local-market brand is finished. Every product will set out to sell in markets other than its country of origin. Broader concepts of quality and style will come into play and Europe will have enormous credibility with consumers everywhere. So although Minale Tattersfield has diversified all over the world, you can see that Europe is clearly the best place for a design company to start.

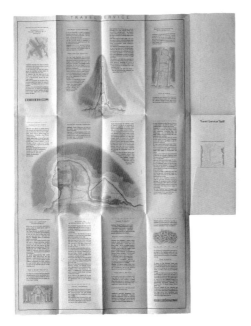

Travel brochure for NatWest Bank. Creating famous localities within a relief map 1987.

COUNTRIES IN EUROPE WHERE MINALE TATTERSFIELD
DESIGN STRATEGY UNDERTAKE THE MAJORITY OF
THEIR DESIGN WORK

CHAPTER SIX

GLOBAL VIEW– SETTING UP AN INTERNATIONAL NETWORK

GLOBAL VIEW

SETTING UP AN INTERNATIONAL NETWORK

Despite the apparent glamour of winning international design commissions, the truth is that most design consultancies don't expand overseas just because they think it would be an exciting thing to do. They are drawn into new markets, some on the other side of the world, because their long-standing clients have developed from local or national companies into multi-national ones.

Basically the world market for design services can be split into three: Europe, North America, and the Pacific Rim. Client demand is the most significant single reason to develop international horizons as a designer. These days few large-scale businesses trade locally or nationally. If your design firm has been building long-term relationships with clients based on confidence and trust, then it is likely that you will be called upon to service their multi-national needs.

But beyond the design markets of mainland Europe, the distances become greater, the cultural variations harder to bridge, and the financial stakes higher. It becomes more difficult to make clear judgements and for that reason I advocate finding local partners with whom you can collaborate. If you have run a tight ship as a design business, and followed my advice earlier in the book, then you will still own 100 per cent of your company and be in a position to exchange equity with those partners. Informal deals of this kind then give you a powerbase and leverage in design markets which would otherwise be alien and remote.

MINALE TATTERSFIELD DESIGN STRATEGY'S INTERNATIONAL NETWORK OUTSIDE EUROPE

CASABLANCA

KUWAIT

TOKYO
OSAKA

HONG KONG

BRISBANE
SYDNEY

FINDING OVERSEAS PARTNERS

I am often asked how I go about choosing suitable international partners for Minale Tattersfield. There is no magic formula and in my case it has involved a process of travelling and meeting people over ten years or more. But from my experience I would say that in 90 per cent of cases, your future partners are the people you meet casually and get to know and like in a social context. I can safely say that if : had been introduced to many of my prospective partners in a formal business context through an agency then it would never have worked. You have to enjoy the company of a person if the partnership is going to function on any meaningful level.

Let me illustrate this point. I met our Australian partner, Brisbane based architect and graphic designer Michael Bryce, by chance, during a lecture tour of Australian art colleges. Together we formed Minale Tattersfield Bryce in 1988 with a view to building on Bryce's strong track record in graphic design for leisure and tourism, often working for prestigious government clients. At the time Australia was booming and the prospects were rosy. Since then, the Land of Oz has suffered one of the most savage economic downturns in its history. This is disappointing, of course, but it doesn't affect our long-term relationship because it is founded on friendship and mutual respect, not hard cash. If our partnership has been forged on economic grounds alone, it would not have been able to survive.

Often things don't turn out how you envisaged they would in new international markets, but if your partnership is rooted in the personal commitment, not coldly calculated on a balance sheet, it will ride out the hard times.

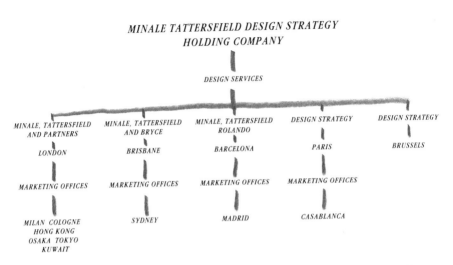

MINALE TATTERSFIELD DESIGN STRATEGY
HOLDING COMPANY

DESIGN SERVICES

MINALE, TATTERSFIELD AND PARTNERS	*MINALE, TATTERSFIELD AND BRYCE*	*MINALE, TATTERSFIELD ROLANDO*	*DESIGN STRATEGY*	*DESIGN STRATEGY*
LONDON	*BRISBANE*	*BARCELONA*	*PARIS*	*BRUSSELS*
MARKETING OFFICES	*MARKETING OFFICES*	*MARKETING OFFICES*	*MARKETING OFFICES*	
MILAN COLOGNE HONG KONG OSAKA TOKYO KUWAIT	*SYDNEY*	*MADRID*	*CASABLANCA*	

Take Hong Kong, where we teamed up with designer and marketing specialist David Liu. Our gameplan was to move into Hong Kong to be close to the industries of mainland China. The Chinese, we reckoned, would be aiming to export to the west and in particular the rich consumer markets of Europe through the gateway of Hong Kong, and they would need a company like Minale Tattersfield to help them get their product and message right.

What actually happened is that the only clients we won there were sophisticated Hong Kong based companies, such as food manufacturer The Garden Company and communication company Cable & Wireless. It is strange how things work out. It certainly underlines my belief that you can't make rigid business plans in international design – you have to take what fate throws your way. It also confirms my view that you can only make headway in markets with industries which can recognise, appreciate and afford sophisticated design.

For that reason, I am less excited about developments in Eastern Europe than many of my peers because I believe it will be another 20 years before they have the economic infrastructure to take what the top international design consultancies have to offer. China is another case in point. A Chinese client in Hong Kong recently contacted us about doing some packaging work. Fine. But when we looked into the enquiry, it transpired that the Chinese government wished to pay us for our services in coal. Not so fine. Unfortunately the coal was still in the ground and we would have to arrange to have it dug up ourselves!

1989: symbol for the Australian National Trust by our partner, Michael Bryce, in Australia.

1990: symbol for The Garden Company, the biggest bakery in Hong Kong.

WORKING IN JAPAN

However the Japanese market has the sophistication, discernment and the wealth to source the best design in the world. Such is the economic power of Japan that its domestic market is one of the most desirable of all to enter. Furthermore the Japanese are great admirers and consumers of European design. Leading Euro-architects, designers and artists such as Aldo Rossi, Nigel Coates and Philippe Starck have been invited to put up buildings there, and the pursuit and purchase of designer "names" has become a serious pastime in Japanese corporate circles.

Against this background, we considered that it was important to have a strong foothold in Japan. Following our introductory

Philippe Starck in Japan.

Photographer B. Marawiec   Architectural Association

cultural exhibition of Minale Tattersfield work at the Axis Gallery in Tokyo in 1988, we were fortunate enough to attract the attention of a major client – Kansai Paints of Osaka. This chemical-industrial giant, which is the roughly the size of ICI in the UK, contacted us to say that it admired our approach. A subsequent commission to design Kansai's corporate identity proved an unbelievable, larger-than-life experience – and a fitting introduction to working in Japan.

Our first presentation was to six top Kansai executives. Our second was to 200 middle managers. Our third was to 15,000 employees at their annual convention in a giant sports stadium. At this event I was flown up in a hot air balloon while the new corporate identity was revealed. I even had to join in a company anthem newly penned by one of Japan's most famous song-writers. And every Kansai presentation was recorded on video by three cameras – the third was there if the first two failed.

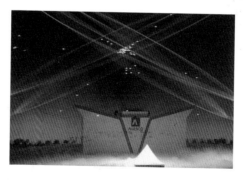

Launching the Alesco corporate identity in front of 15,000 employees!

*Work for Alesco
corporate identity
in Japan 1989.*

DEALING WITH JAPANESE CULTURE

The publicity that surrounded the launch of the new Kansai identity meant that work subsequently snowballed for us in Japan with commissions from Toyota, Fuji and *saké* maker Sawanotsuru. Japan has now become a more familiar place for us – clients there especially like *Japonesque*, a European interpretation of Japanese style. But the culture still has the capacity to jolt.

For instance, I recall travelling with my good friend and assistant David Turner on the Tokyo underground system. As we progressed, station titles had subheadings in English and we felt all was well with the world. Suddenly those reassuring subheadings stopped and we were horribly lost. We arrived at our client meeting two-and-a-half hours late but when we explained the reason why, the Japanese were very understanding.

The episode reminded me of the time the Pentagram designer Alan Fletcher rented a car in Greece, in 1968, bought a map and drove for 50 miles before becoming totally lost. His map had all the names in capitals while the road signs were all in upper and lower case. He just couldn't match the Greek letters up!

Often it is the little things which can really disconcert you. As a European, I have never been able to get used to the lack of space in Japan. I will always remember travelling to Japan for the launch of the Kansai identity with my wife Roberta: the company pulled out all the stops with first class air travel and a booking in a top hotel. We were allocated a suite which is unusual in Japan, but I assumed we were honoured guests.

Minale Tattersfield's proposal for the new Toyota corporate identity in 1990.

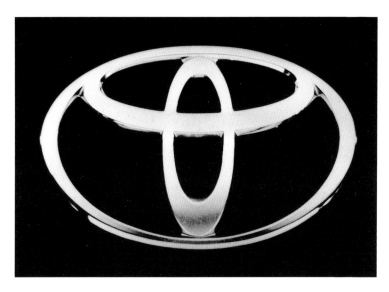

The final symbol from Nippon Design which bears a strong resemblance!

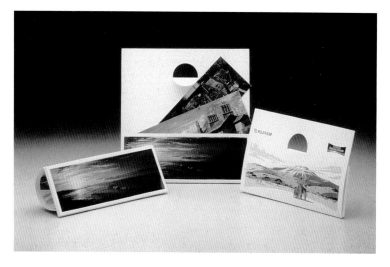

1991: this design by Minale Tattersfield for Fuji photo wallet also becomes a photo frame.

The next day I awoke from a deep sleep and heard rustling in the adjoining room to our bedroom. Who could be in our suite? I opened the door to find 20 Japanese journalists waiting to interview me, microphones and pens at the ready – and I was standing aghast in my pyjamas. So that's why they gave me a suite!

On another occasion I visited a Geisha house in Kobi to watch the *Maiko* – the apprentice Geisha – sing and dance. We had to sit for hours cross-legged on the floor and were served drinks at a long, low table. It was supposed to be a relaxing, entertaining experience. Instead, unaccustomed to the lack of space to stretch out and move around, my legs went to sleep. They were locked solid and, embarrassingly, three men had to lift me up and carry me out of the place.

DO'S AND DON'T IN JAPAN

From my experiences in Japan, I have compiled a list of do's and don'ts when dealing with Japanese executives.

DO
· Always bring a good stock of business cards.
· Always learn the client's corporate anthem, or be able to mime it well. (This is a sure way to win the contract).
· Be prepared to get drunk and/or impress them with a little number on the Karaokie machine.
· Be patient.
· Never take yes as a positive answer.

DON'T
· Lie about your age. You will probably be asked within the first five minutes of every meeting, so get your story straight at the outset.
· Use humour. (The only humour they like is black humour, but be careful how you use it).
· Expect 12 hours' grace if you send a fax as you leave your UK office in the evening. You can guarantee that it will be answered within 30 minutes even if it is 4am in Japan.
· Forget to bring a personal gift for the chairman and his wife.
· Be logical with the Japanese. They only seem satisfied by an illogical explanation.

If this last piece of advice appears strange and at odds with what you may have learnt elsewhere about Japanese business, then let me give you an example. On a recent project for Sawanotsuru, the *saké* (rice wine) company, we were asked to design a new symbol for the organisation. Sawanotsuru means, literally, "rice and Crane (bird)". So we devised a logo showing the wing of the Crane. However when we presented the solution to the client, the explanation we gave – "a marshland scene in the morning seen in the right frame of mind" – was far more acceptable to them.

1991: a marshland scene in the morning seen in the right frame of mind!

Many of the guidelines I apply to dealing with Japanese clients could well be usefully adapted to other clients along the Pacific Rim, most notably in Korea or Singapore. We have never worked there, but we did recently get an interesting enquiry from Singapore – or to be more precise, the Singapore Police Department.

It seems there was a murder in Singapore and the only thing found by detectives in a burnt out car at the scene of the crime was a green plastic plaque with the inscription "Designed by Minale Tattersfield, London" on it. Had the murderers left a calling card? Detectives traced us to London and wanted to know if we had an alibi. Initially there was anxiety all round, but the mystery was solved when we realised what the plaque was.

Unbelievably, it was the bottom of a BP oil container we had designed, which is sold throughout the world. In return for a slight reduction in our fee, we had negotiated for BP to allow us to put a small design credit on the bottom of the oil container. It got us into trouble and as of writing, I still await our first legal, decent and honest commission in Singapore!

The clue for the murder in Singapore is on the bottom of the BP oil can.

AVOIDING AMERICA

Alongside the rich potential of Japan, many designers also see the streets of New York and Los Angeles as paved with gold. I know I am swimming against the tide of popular opinion when I say that the multi-disciplinary design firm should avoid the American market at all costs. I have done a lot of research in this area and I always return from my fact-finding missions horrified by what I have found.

America is not so much the land of opportunity but the land of segmentation. There aren't just packaging specialists, there are cosmetic packaging specialists. There are firms which design cherry jam but never touch marmalade jars! I know I exaggerate but the point is that design markets in the US are so rigid and rooted in 'specialisms' that there is no room for the so-called free spirit to range across the disciplines. And I bet there won't be room if you wait 100 years either. Little wonder that there are no truly multi-disciplinary design firms in the States: the character of the market would not allow any to survive intact.

So, I suggest that you steer well clear of America. Plenty of British design firms invested in the US design market in the 1980s – the cost of all the mergers and takeover amounted to around £70 million, I believe – but nearly all got badly burnt. Some UK consultancies even signed their own death warrant by moving into the US. Their experiences should serve as a warning.

THE KUWAIT INVASION

Of course, you can have the best advice in the world and make the most careful plans. But in practice things rarely turn out the way your rational analysis predicted they would. That is why I believe the opposite to the standard dictum of business practice – that good managers must plan ahead. I have discovered that business strategy is all about coincidence and business deals all about friendship. The random factor cannot be eliminated and I have a good example to demonstrate this.

I listened to advice on how to expand our business in the Gulf. I was told we needed a systematic plan for the Middle East. So once we had work for Caterpillar in Saudi Arabia and the Commercial Bank of Kuwait and other financial institutions in Kuwait, we decided that the time was right to open a Kuwaiti office. We spent two years searching for the right local partner and eventually found Sami Al-Ebrahim, a former Minister of Information in the Kuwaiti government.

After signing all the papers, and giving our new partner 51 per cent of our design company in Kuwait, as laid down by terms in the Gulf, we assessed the future. Successive trips and extensive lobbying had secured three major projects: a new corporate identity for the Kuwaiti Transport Company; packaging for the Danish-Kuwaiti Dairy Board; and the design of all the festivities for the 30th anniversary of Kuwait's independence. (For this last scheme we designed a string of pearls to adorn the sky comprising 30 giant balloons and a laser light show projecting from Failaka island onto Kuwait City).

K·P·T·C شِـركَة النَقلْ العَـام الكُويتَـيّة

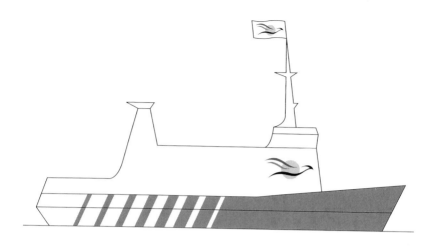

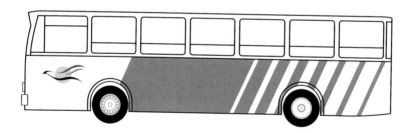

Kuwait transport company corporate identity, presented two weeks after the liberation.

Having signed the deal, I went on holiday to the south of France a very satisfied man. I had done the right thing in Kuwait and could sunbathe in peace. Now as a rule, I never buy a newspaper on holiday. But one day in early August 1990 I succumbed to the temptation of the *Nice Matin*. I opened the paper and the headline immediately hit me: "IRAQ INVADES KUWAIT".

We wrote to our new Kuwait office to find out what was happening under Iraqi occupation but the letter only went as far as the sorting office in Twickenham a couple of miles away before being returned to our Richmond office. At the time of writing, Kuwait is now liberated and we are slowly picking up the pieces of our design company. In fact we aim to play a significant role in the reconstruction of that war-torn country, especially through our Transpartners transport design consortium. But the Kuwait office episode just goes to show that you can make all the right moves and the accidents of fate will still ensure that all your good work will be undone – or at least postponed to a later date.

A POSITIVE INTERNATIONAL APPROACH

Given the climate of rapid change in world design, there can only be one or two core principles to observe. First, if you sit and do nothing, then nothing will happen. You have to keep trying lots of initiatives in the hope that one or two will succeed. My advice is to plant lot of seeds: some will die but some will flourish, even – as in the case of Kuwait – it takes a long time and you temporarily give up hope. Second, you can help to foster a positive international culture within your design company by employing designers from all over the world. Minale Tattersfield has always done this: we speak seven different languages in our head office and one of our partners, Nobuoki Ohtani, is from Japan.

But in the final analysis, the speed of economic, technological, political and social change will always upset the best-laid plans of the design consultant. Who in business consultancy could have predicted the pace of *perestroika* in the Soviet Union? Which City analyst could have anticipated that the Red Army generals of Reagan's "Evil Empire" would be quizzed mercilessly by the American TV networks every night on the steps of Kremlin!

It is the USSR which provides the backdrop for my favourite international design story. In the 1970s a friend of mine, the photographer Tony Evans, flew into Moscow to do a reportage job. At passport control, he joined a queue of some 200 people and estimated that it would take at least an hour to get through. Suddenly two men smartly dressed like private detectives approached him, whisked him through customs, and drove him in a big black car straight to his hotel down the central lane reserved for top party officials. Evans was completely baffled at this (red) star treatment. Inside his hotel room, he put his case on the bed and scratched his head mystified. Then he noticed the initials of the logo on the brand name of his case. They read: KGB.

CHAPTER SEVEN

MONEY MATTERS – KEEPING THE BANK HAPPY

MONEY MATTERS

KEEPING THE BANK HAPPY

Some designers make the mistake of thinking that if they put commercial interests above all else, then money matters will automatically turn out right. I believe the opposite is true: if designers stick to the main objective of designing then they are more likely to prosper. Why? My reasoning is simple. Every designer I have ever known who has gone all out with the prime objective to make as much money as possible has either ended up bankrupt or close to it.

Naked financial ambition is ill-suited to an industry which is cyclical. The peaks and troughs come in waves – recession will follow boom time as surely as night follows day. If you only want to sell design as marketing tool for maximum gain then the waves will be very deep and dangerous. You will rise on the crest of a wave and sell out your stake for a fortune only to be swept away later on a tidal wave of debt.

That is why I strongly believe that a gentle, steady growth in turnover over a number of years is a greater guarantee of success than a meteoric rise with turnover doubling and quadrupling practically overnight. A sudden surge in a design business is often a prelude to doom. A design firm cannot absorb and digest that amount of growth because the output in what is essentially a craft business cannot be cranked up sufficiently to cope.

The growth chart of Minale Tattersfield shows only a very gradual rise in turnover over a number of years. Compared to some other high-flying (and crashing) design firms, this growth has been barely perceivable. But the steadiness and gentleness

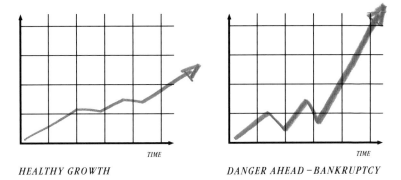

TIME

TIME

HEALTHY GROWTH   *DANGER AHEAD - BANKRUPTCY*

of that rise has enabled us to manage change prudently and has provided the basis for our continued success.

AVOIDING THE FINANCIAL PITFALLS

A low growth rate is just one of my recommendations if you want to keep the bank manager happy in the long term. As I have discussed elsewhere, you should only diversify within design consultancy – avoid a move into manufacturing like the plague! You should also expand through an exchange of equity to build an international network rather than paying hard cash to acquire companies.

Looking back, I realise that if we had put ourselves in the position whereby we had to buy all the partners who are now in the Minale Tattersfield Design Strategy international network, we would have gone out of business. Instead we used the rich reserves of equity within the company to fund expansion. In that context, my initial advice that you should steer clear of investors or backers becomes more relevant. We hadn't surrendered any of our company so we had something to play with when the time came to expand around the world.

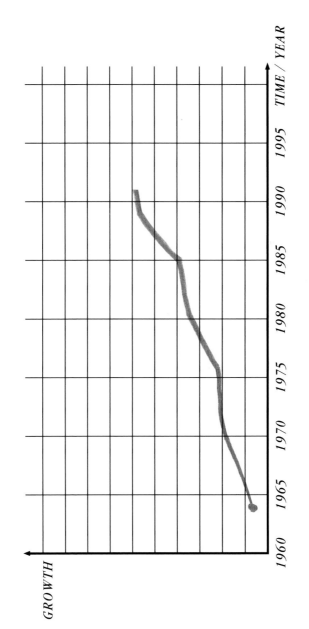

Another pitfall to avoid is the bank loan. If you are patient and take a long-term view of your business, you shouldn't need to borrow money. Design doesn't require enormous financial outlay; it requires a certain sangfroid. As a designer you are no security on a loan because you have no absolute guarantee of future work. The pattern of design work is completely arbitrary which is what makes it so exciting, I suppose.

Minale Tattersfield has never taken out bank loans even though our bank, National Westminster, happens to be one of our biggest clients. At least we know the cheque is not going to bounce!

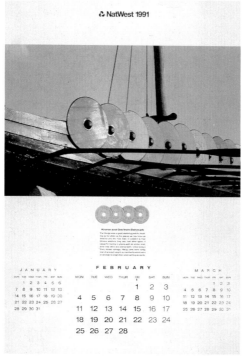

A page from NatWest Calender 1991 linking
Scandinavian coins with the Vikings.

BALANCING THE BOOKS

It has now become a political cliche after the era of Margaret Thatcher, but you should run your design company like a corner shop. For that you must put aside just 30 minutes a month. This task cannot be done by your secretary or your accountant or your financial advisor. It must be done by you.

The procedure is simple. Calculate your overheads – how much it is costing to run the company in wages, rent and so on. Then collect all your invoices for that month, subtract the costs and add up all the fees charged. If your fee income exceeds your outgoings then you are in profit. Hooray! If your outgoings outstrip your fee income, you are making a loss and you must take corrective action if you want to survive.

Every month I know precisely the financial position of Minale Tattersfield by following this routine. I put an entire year's financial performance on one sheet of paper. If you do the same, then at the end of the year you can match up your figures to those produced by your accountant.

Assessing costs and fees this way, I have discovered that there is no continuity whatsoever in monthly turnover in the design business. It is an entirely arbitrary universe, as I have said. One February will be brilliant, the next year February will be a disaster. You cannot plan for a busy time of year – financial purple patches don't repeat themselves in sequence. The pattern is random. A designer is only as good as his last job. And any entrepreneur who buys a design firm cannot control it in any meaningful statistical way because you cannot predict profitability in the design field.

CHASING BAD DEBTS

However, despite the vagaries of the design profession, I have not been troubled unduly with bad debts. In fact I have had only one bad debt of £250 in 25 years in business. We even bought a building from the gentleman in question who owed us the money, and afterwards I still pursued him for the cheque! He was amazed that even after concluding such a big property deal with him, I should still be so persistent about a small amount. But I always pursue money vigorously, if it is rightly mine. It is when the designer has not followed the correct procedures and is not in the right that all the trouble starts with client debts.

Chasing bad debts is a waste of time and, yes, money. But it is on the increase. 25 years ago I used to do jobs based on mutual trust and send in an invoice on a wing and a prayer. Now the practice of estimating and invoicing is much more rigorous.

THE PERILS OF FREE PITCHING

The surest way to crash out of business is to abandon yourself to the Russian Roulette of what is known in the design business as "free pitching" – producing unpaid speculative creative work in the hope of winning the job. This is gambling in its purest form and you are sure to lose in the end. Forget the ethics and just look at the practicalities. If you enter three unpaid pitches for work, you will on the law of averages win one. But the benefit of this single success will be outweighed by the costs of chasing after the other two with speculative designs that bump up studio overheads.

Ban free pitches – it is an insult to designers and ultimately the client will suffer with a substandard solution.

Free pitching arose because too many design firms expanded too rapidly. They were left with too many mouths to feed and too little work, so they became desperate. They thought that they had the people in the studio anyway so they may as well produce some speculative designs to spice up the presentation. Then some clients came to expect it as part of the pitch for their business. My advice is to watch staff numbers closely. Run a tight ship and keep your designers to a minimum so that you only need to take on the work you are offered without having to enter a ludicrous and costly lottery.

Free pitching is an abuse of client power and an insult to designers. Those design firms who persist in seeking work via this route will always be in the third division of the design industry. How can you produce a piece of relevant design when you don't know the context of the problem and haven't discussed a brief?

The only exception I would make is the architectural competition. This a time-honoured way for architects to win work. It is also a platform for new artistic and avant garde ideas. If the architects win, they stand to benefit from a large contract for a building or environment with a value that can withstand entry in half-a-dozen more architectural competitions. But graphic designers, constantly competing for small-budget brochure and packaging jobs, will soon start failing if it costs enormously to win every new job via the free pitching route.

BE YOUR OWN LANDLORD

Property costs are also responsible for sinking design firms without trace. The worst cases are usually associated with studios in voguish city areas such as Covent Garden or Soho in London: the rents start as inexpensive but then climb steeply. Many designers simply end up working for the landlord. So my advice is to buy your own building as soon as you can afford it.

Your building must express your personality as a designer. It is an essential part of your creative identity. Even if you are renting a space, you will want to rip up the carpet tiles, remove the fluorescent strips and remodel the room. So if you are saddled with the expense of changing the environment anyway, why not do it in a building you own? A mortgage is preferable to a tenancy – even if it means you should look outside the centre of a city at less obvious areas to locate your design business.

WHAT FEES TO CHARGE

Unlike architects, the design profession in Britain is precluded from publishing official fee scales. So deciding what fees to charge becomes part of your personal judgement and developing maturity as a designer.

I believe that you mustn't sell design too cheaply. Many clients feel proud that they have approached a leading design consultant for a solution and would be disappointed not to pay a premium for it. Clients *expect* to pay for quality. If you undercharge, then the solution can be tarnished in the minds of some patrons of design. But the real issue is about producing excellent design. The fee structure is a marginal issue. Money is a consequence of a means to an end. In design it cannot be the end in itself.

1986: original presentation for the bottle, label and name of the new alcohol-free product – Eisberg. This design is an example of a success story where money was invested in design. This solution would never come from a free pitch!

MULTI-DISCIPLINARY FLEXIBILITY

There is a myth about the multi-disciplinary workings of a design consultancy that I would like to dispel. During the 1980s some publicly quoted design firms used their multi-disciplinary basis as an excuse for poor financial results. Their argument was that with at least three separate methods of payment – hourly studio rates for graphic design, royalties on sales for product design, and a percentage of overall spend for environmental design – it was difficult to keep control of cash flow.

DESIGN SERVICES: OVERALL BREAKDOWN OF SPECIFIC DESIGN FIELDS

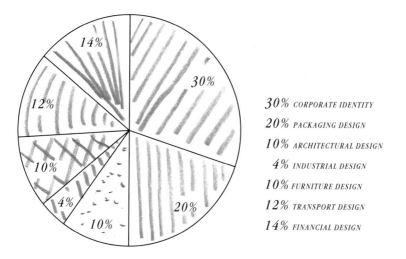

30% CORPORATE IDENTITY
20% PACKAGING DESIGN
10% ARCHITECTURAL DESIGN
 4% INDUSTRIAL DESIGN
10% FURNITURE DESIGN
12% TRANSPORT DESIGN
14% FINANCIAL DESIGN

A multi-disciplinary design consultancy can solve all these different problems successfully by cross-referencing their design skills.

But I would argue that having a multi-disciplinary character to a design business *helps* cash flow rather than hinders it by providing far more flexibility. Design markets are subject to constant fluctuations, as I have explained. But in a multi-disciplinary design practice, when interior design is down, corporate identity will be up; when architectural graphics are down, industrial design will be up; and so on. At Minale Tattersfield, our design services in specific fields are broken down in such a way that we are usually covered. I believe that one-track design specialists are harder hit in a recession than the multi-disciplinary practice because they have nowhere to switch to if their chosen sector suffers a downturn.

But if you want to keep your options open in a multi-disciplinary environment then you must employ design all-rounders who can respond to different problem-solving challenges. If you recruit only packaging specialists, then you will have to keep finding packaging commissions to keep them busy. You will be forced to feed a machine irrespective of whether there is demand for packaging design out there at the time.

At Minale Tattersfield, our partners have core 'specialisms' – for instance, Nobuoki Ohtani heads industrial design and Nigel Mac-Fall is the interior design partner – but all our young designers gain broad experience. It is not unusual for a graphic-trained designer to work on an interior or furniture-based project.

I believe that a multi-disciplinary design firm can always solve the large and complex problems – a rail network or shopping environment, for example – in a fresher and more rational way because it can gain an insight through the contribution of professionals in a variety of adjacent design fields. There is a richness in overlapping expertise which enables the design team to take a short cut to the solution. And gradually, over time, the multi-disciplinary design group can offer a larger portfolio in every specialism than even the specialists themselves.

What has multi-disciplinary flexibility got to do with money matters? Everything. I believe that commerce and industry now prefer to commission consultants with a broad span of knowledge and expertise. The client is the specialist – and wants his problem assessed by an expert who can take a wider, more lateral view. Far from leading to financial ruin, the multi-disciplinary route can lead to design riches – and keep the bank happy.

MINALE TATTERSFIELD MANAGEMENT STRUCTURE

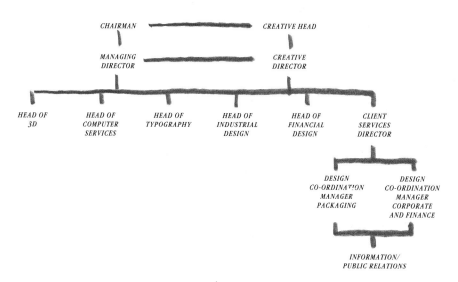

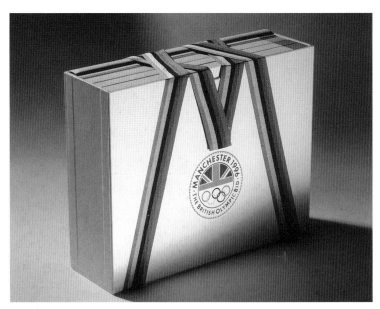

Multi-design projects: Manchester Olympic Bid 1990. Flexi stool 1985. Interior design for Stockmann in Finland 1989. Corporate identity for Italian silk manufacturer Mantero, 1989.

MANTERO ᵛᴵᴵᴵ

CHAPTER EIGHT

HANDING OVER – HOW TO PLAN THE SUCCESSION

HOW TO PLAN THE SUCCESSION

I believe that there are two clearly defined segments to your professional life as a designer: in the first part, you do it; in the second part, you teach others how to do it. After you have been in business 20 years or more you will have reached the stage when you'll have done everything you want to do. At this stage you must spend your time teaching others how to do it and lining up the next generation to carry the torch of your design practice.

Again, I make the analogy with sport. After playing a sport for a number of years, the most satisfying thing is to coach others. In design, unless you devote time to teaching others then your consultancy will die with you. I have always preached this philosophy at Minale Tattersfield where we have lined up successive generations to follow in our wake.

In the first generation are stalwarts such as Alex Maranzano, Ian Grindle and Nigel Mac-Fall who have been with Brian and I for 15 to 20 years. They are now partners in the practice. In the second generation are valued company members such as Ian Delaney, Dimitri Karavis and Marian Hawkins who have been with us for 10 to 12 years. There is even a third generation of staff – people like Frances McGee and Susan Smith – who can claim five years' association with Minale Tattersfield.

This is an enviable structure in terms of continuity and loyalty, and I feel sure it will enable the company to continue to prosper long after Brian and I have retired. How many other design firms can claim such a staff structure? We have only achieved it by following a number of inviolate principles. The most important has been a policy of steady, unspectacular growth rather than

The Partners and Associates of Minale Tattersfield Design Strategy Group at our annual conference in Richmond 1989.

forcing the pace. If we had engineered a more sudden upswing in fortunes, the company would have become a more volatile place. Staff would have become dissatisfied, management problems would have ensued, resignations would have been rife, and all sense of continuity would have been lost. I am sure you know the pattern from observing other design firms.

It also goes back to selecting designers with the right educational, cultural and personal background who can flourish in a multi-disciplinary environment. If they can switch from one design specialism to another so that boredom and dissatisfaction doesn't set in, you can then retain your staff for a long time by offering new challenges at regular intervals.

A COHERENT PHILOSOPHY

I have discovered over the years that people won't rock the boat if you give them a coherent design philosophy in which they can believe. They won't walk out and betray a set of ideals which they have been sharing for a number of years. Of course young designers with fresh ideas will always influence the venerable founders of a well-known design company; it has happened often at Minale Tattersfield. But the successful design practice must also stamp a coherent philosophy on its business so that staff can *believe* in something and commit their creative energies to tangible and defined objectives.

Design firms will only make a mark if everyone pulls in the same direction. The reason why so many large design companies don't survive in the long term is because they fail to develop a coherent philosophy which embraces all aspects of design practice. As a result, their staff lack commitment even on the most basic level.

Consistency of outlook is all-important. Some people say that you can't do the same thing all your life. I disagree. Your vision may evolve, but I believe that the core principles with which you begin your professional career won't change as that career progresses and will never change. You can test this thesis immediately by asking yourself whether or not you would be ashamed to show work you did 10 or 20 years ago. If you can show the work without making excuses then you must have been doing something right all along. The trouble is that too many designers are apologetic about material in their portfolio.

They make comments like..."This is not very good. I did it four years ago. My ideas have moved on a lot since then." I have no sympathy whatsoever with this attitude.

My own ideas about design have not changed one iota since I first formulated a philosophy of problem-solving as a young designer. Nobody I have met in my professional life has challenged my beliefs to the extent that I have been forced to radically rethink my rationale. In that time I have lived through some powerful and vivid movements in design: the pop-art 1960s of Mr Freedom and Alan Aldridge; the whole earth 1970s; and the post-modern and deconstructivist 1980s in which, to paraphrase Tom Wolfe, everyone dived into the great walk-in closet of design history to dress up in different historical styles.

I have lived through Flower Power, Memphis, High Tech Style, Recession Chic, Soviet Constructivism, Bauhaus Revivalism and Acid House – and none of these stylistic movements has convinced me that my original beliefs were anything other than absolutely right. Of course, as a designer, I have dabbled with these movements at different times to reflect the spirit of the age in which I have been working, and also, if I am honest, to feed the media monster. Design journalists love these new trends (functionalism is an old, old story): what else would they have to write about?

But if you are a butterfly you will have a short summer. Designers who simply leap from one fashion trend to the next are essentially shallow people. What they are producing is superficial design and I don't believe it is possible to build a long term business around it. There is another point to be made here.

Soviet Constructivism is 'in vogue' now, but for how long?

Heads of design firms who mark themselves out as dedicated followers of fashion run the risk of being labelled hopeless has-beens by their young staff as soon as they miss a cue. Far better to make it known that you are above such transitory trends, so you can never been accused of being out of tune with the times.

At Minale Tattersfield we have taken elements of every new fad that has come along to communicate at the time. But we have always turned the current style in vogue to our own advantage rather than slavishly copying it. I am also arrogant enough to believe that we have often been ahead of the trends.

LETTING GO

A lot of people say that letting go of the company you have founded is very hard to do. I think it is the easiest thing in the world. Those designers who think that if they walk out then everything will collapse have a false perception of what it is all about. If you have followed all the right procedures in running your design business, then it won't collapse when you step out of it. It will continue to function smoothly (or at least as smoothly as any design organisation can ever function!)

The important principle about letting go is to prepare for it properly and do it in stages. Establish a share option scheme for key staff so that one day they will own the company. Make sure that you don't have so many partners that they can vote you out or buy you out. I only had one partner at Minale Tattersfield for many years: Brian could never afford to buy me out and *vice versa*. Now we have nine partners.

At the time of writing, I have signalled my intention to step down very soon as chairman of Minale Tattersfield. I will remain a senior partner. Alex Maranzano, representing the next generation, will step up into the chairman's role. I am 52, still in the driving seat, and I want to let go while still relatively young. I don't want to flog myself until I am 65.

One of my heroes is the great engineer Sir Ove Arup who handled the question of succession in his multi-disciplinary practice brilliantly. He let go of control in progressive steps and was still attending meetings and giving valued advice when he was 90.

I think it is a privilege to be welcomed inside a design business at 90 and Arup is unquestionably my role model. Once I have handed on the baton I will bite the bullet when my successor as chairman makes a decision I don't agree with. I will only offer advice when asked to do so. And I will adhere to a long-established Minale Tattersfield tenet: that you should never criticise a person's work without offering an alternative solution. My intention is to make sure I am still a welcome face around the place for many years to come. That way I can live happily ever after while someone else takes the strain in the daily frontline of managing the company.

THE FUTURE FOR DESIGNERS

Just as the design profession has changed dramatically during the past 25 years I have been in practice, so it is set for further radical transformations ahead. The only difference will be in the hugely accelerated pace of change which will call into question the very nature of the designer's contribution. A time of reckoning is just around the corner for all of us as design consultants.

I believe that the designer of the future will be more of an explorer, inventor and street-wise adventurer than the current professional jealously guarding the boundaries of a vocational craft. This is because it will be necessary for the products and services of the future to be *discovered* by consumers rather than designed and presented to them as at present. Marketing is set to become much more subtle, elusive and intangible and the value and role of design within the marketing mix will have to change also.

Statistical targeting of socio-economic groups and conscious use of design elements to achieve those objectives will be replaced by such random, abstract values as discovery and coincidence. Marketing will start whispering as opposed to shouting – and designers will be forced to find a new voice for a new age. Already this is beginning to happen. Many international sales successes have sprung up as if from nowhere. Analyse the reasons for their success and you can draw no logical conclusions. You can't really imitate the product or recreate the conditions of its launch because the values associated with it are so intangible. I first noticed this phenomenon with the popularity of pilot (aviator) sunglasses in the 1950s.

Why were Fruit of the Loom T-shirts so successful? Or TAG Heuer watches, San Pellegrino water, or Doc Martens boots? Because they were *discovered* by consumers rather than presented to

Doc Martens, Fruit of the Loom, San Pellegrino water, Ray-Ban sunglasses, Tag Heuer watch – some examples of items that have become successful through 'discovery'!

the market on a plate by marketeers. The whisper went around and the product caught on. As consumers we all feel happier making our own discoveries, rather than being manipulated *en masse* by large media budgets. The Scottish soft drink Irn Bru has the same "street" credibility which could over time make it a popular "discovery" throughout Europe. I believe that people will discover and use brands and products like they discover a particular bistro, science fiction writer or poet – choices of objects in particular will be personal, subjective and coincidental, rather than based on a regimented, segmented brand loyalty.

A WORLD OF DISCOVERY

The Alessi lemon squeezer designed by Philippe Starck is a prime example of this new design world of discovery. You can't immediately discern what this extraordinary object is. You only pick it up through the whisper on the grapevine. The Japanese understand this discovery principle well and are beginning to use it in a highly sophisticated way. Unless the western design industry enters the world of discovery then today's designers will become professional dinosaurs in the twenty-first century.

The new Nissan 'Figaro' – the Japanese are now looking back to be able to go forward.

Even within my own design company, similar principles have been applied to market our own product. Our Scribble trademark was discovered by many people in the 1960s. They found it intriguing and wanted to know more about us. Today, of course, the design world is full of freehand squiggles and brushstroke symbols and nobody wants to discover them any more. But in our projects we have always tried to build in an element of discovery into the design so that people can find things out for themselves.

CHRISTIES
ESTATE AGENTS

A small discovery. The 'C' of Christies becomes the moat of the Englishman's Castle 1989.

We even pushed this concept to its furthest extent with a proposal that British Petroleum should position its gas stations underground in country areas. The only sign of a petrol filling station from the road would be a discrete sign. Our thinking was that in a sector in which there is absolutely no brand loyalty whatsoever (motorists just stop at whatever gas station is on the road), BP could offer its customers a sense of discovery and identify itself with the environmental lobby, by not spoiling country vistas with ugly gas stations.

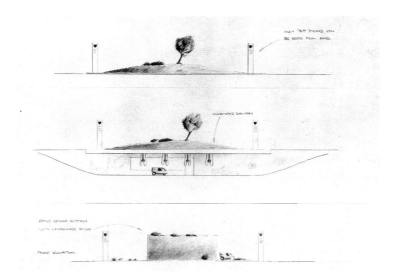

*One of our proposals (not accepted) for BP's 'environmentally friendly'
petrol station. In the countryside all the unslightly activities are
contained underground.*

Our concept was turned down flat by the client (BP's gesture to
the environment stretched only as far as painting its petrol
stations green), but such ideas will surely catch on as we move
further into a world of discovery. The important dimension of
the client-designer relationship will be to give consumers sights
and sensations they have never experienced before. That will
require designers to use their brains in 360 degree turns,
thinking laterally to produce unexpected solutions.

My criticism of design education and design practice as it
currently stands is that designers are only choosing to use their
brains in 90 degree turns. The solutions of the future are
unlikely to arrive via existing design methodology – they
will come from science, technology, the street, anthropology.

*Two memorable landscapes: the 'Energy Farm' and the ship on the
mountain in 'Fitzcarraldo' (overleaf).*

The aim will be to create a new landscape. We are set for an
interesting time.

I remember once chancing across a scene in California at a
place called Energy Farm. There, two thousand white wind
generators gleamed in a radically new man-made landscape
that no other generation has ever seen. It was a landscape I
had never seen before in my life, though I have travelled all
over the world, and it was a powerful emotional discovery.
It epitomised the essence of what design in the future must
offer – a revelation of completely new landscapes, relationships, experiences and emotions. Only once before had I
experienced a similar sensation – the scene in Werner Herzog's
epic film *Fitzcarraldo* in which an ocean liner is led
incongruously seen moving up the side of a mountain.

In a sense my whole career has been about discovery, even if one or two of them have been uncomfortable realisations of ghastly mistakes. It has taken me at least 25 years to write this book. I had to live it to write it, but my final tip is that having absorbed all the advice I have offered, don't follow any of it. Tomorrow it will all be different and you will have to plot your own path for your multi-disciplinary design company in radically changing times. So good luck and just one thing – wait at least a quarter-century before you tell people how you did it.

SYDNEY 2OOO

A powerful work by Minale, Tattersfield & Bryce for the Sydney 2000 Olympic Bid

*Corporate Identity
for London
Transport Museum
and the Eurostar
train. Spanning
the gap of 100 years
of transport.*

**London Transport
Museum**

Bluewater
KENT

*type for
water Kent,
ga retail
lopment of
5,000 sq. metres
e biggest in
pe!*

*The proof of a
good design:
a new product
with a new bottle
shape which has
captured a big
share of the
premium gin
market without
a single penny
being spent on
advertising.*

*International design.
Ice Tea for
Switzerland
and energy drink
for Thailand.*

BOLTON
GROUP

he strength at the base of a column portrays the strength of the international Bolton Group.

BOLTON
GROUP

**NORTHERN
DAIRIES**

*I consider this work
for Northern
Dairies our best
corporate identity
for 1996.*

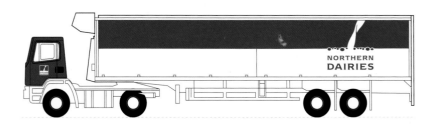

Northern Dairies Limited
Smisby Road
Ashby De La Zouch
Leicestershire
LE65 2UF

Tel: 0530 412858
Fax: 0530 411237

NORTHERN
DAIRIES

Ashby Dairy Company a trading division of Dale Farm Dairy Group Limited
Registered Office: Beverly House, Hull, East Yorkshire HU1 3XG Registered in England number 2361019

Northern Dairies Limited
Smisby Road
Ashby De La Zouch
Leicestershire
LE65 2UF

Tel: 0530 412858
Fax: 0530 411237

S.R Hedge
General Manager

NORTHERN
DAIRIES

Northern Dairies Limited
Smisby Road
Ashby De La Zouch
Leicestershire
LE65 2UF

Tel: 0530 412858
Fax: 0530 411237

With compliments

NORTHERN
DAIRIES

ROYAL ARMOURIES MUSEUM

Royal Armouries Museum corporate identity and signage system. The symbol is based on one of the most extraordinary objects in the collection - a grotesque horned helmet, from a suit of armour made for Henry VIII by the Court Armourer of Maximilian I.

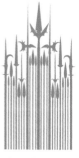

HALL OF STEEL

ORIENTAL

EDUCATION

DOWN

UP

WAR

New corporate identity and industrial design for the biggest textile machine that Minale Tattersfield has ever designed!!

limited Store - Kuwait.

*Interior design for a
retail concept selling
Americana from
Disney to sports.*

London Dial·a·Ride

don Transport
ice for the
rly, Dial-a-Ride.

Packaging design for Kuwait Danish Dairy. Good design is appreciated and understood all over the world.

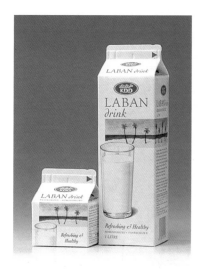

Packaging for San Pellegrino, Italy.

THE F.A. PREMIER LEAGUE

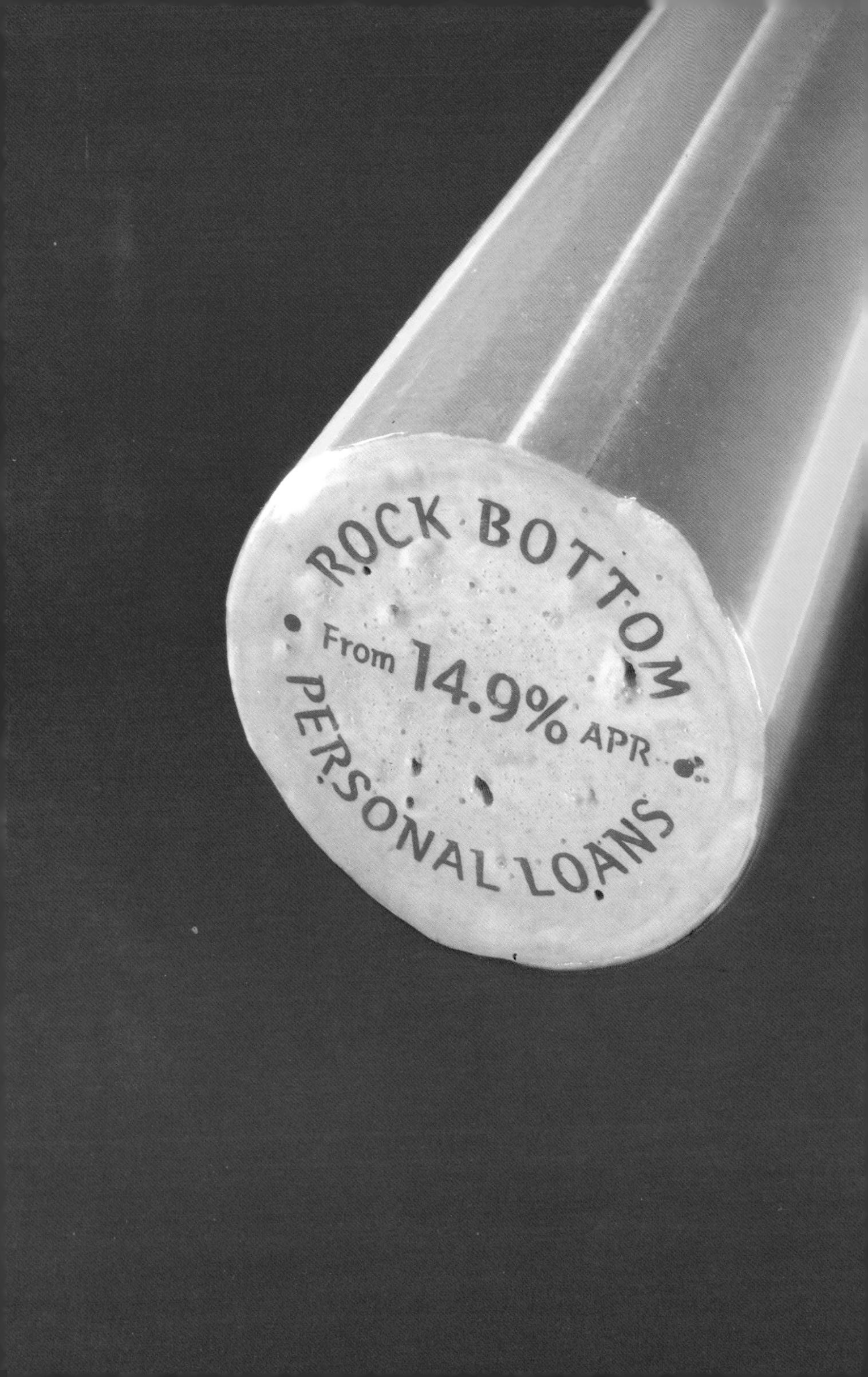
ROCK BOTTOM
From 14.9% APR
PERSONAL LOANS

K BOTTOM
npaign for
est bank
mote a rate
unt.
unday Times
ed to it as
affest canpaign
year' (although
only January).
npact on the
c, however, has
excellent, with
ponse rate up
on the
ous year.

Literature for the Bank of China,
a prestigious job.

BANK OF CHINA

*Latest work by
Minale Tattersfield
& Acton for Thaioil,
Thailand -
corporate identity
and petrol station
design.*

Also by Minale,
Tattersfield & Acton
for Repsol in Spain.
These photos show
the prototype for
testing purposes
under construction.

*Hammersmith
Underground
Station, used by 40
million passengers
a year - now open!*

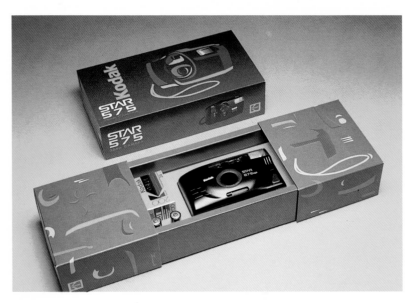

International packaging for Kodak...

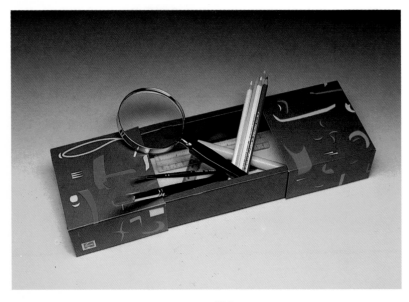

...reusable!

CHAPTER NINE

SURVIVING THE RECESSION – CUTTING BACK

SURVIVING THE RECESSION

CUTTING BACK AND HANGING ON

Surprise, surprise. I haven't stepped down. I haven't handed over the baton to the next generation. I'm still here. When I wrote at the end of the last chapter five years ago that "tomorrow it will all be different" I had no idea just how different it would be. Retirement was no longer an option almost as soon as I'd written that I was about to ease out of the driving seat. The reason why I'm still around – still running the consultancy more than 30 years after I co-founded it – can be summed up in one word. Recession. It has changed the design business totally and completely. It rewrote all the rules. It imposed the toughest operating conditions I have ever experienced in my entire career. In that kind of traumatic climate, could I abandon ship? No way. It needed all the experience and vision we could muster to guide us through.

We survived the recession and this chapter explains how we managed it. It took luck as well as judgement. But we didn't survive unscathed. Nobody did. Any company paying salaries and rent was destined to suffer in the early 1990s when the economy went into steep decline and the recession felt as though it would last forever. For design companies, the pain was especially intense as design budgets were invariably the first to be slashed. It was very painful to tell designers who had worked skillfully and loyally for us for ten years or more that we could no longer afford to keep them. As a company in the UK we went from 60 to 35 people very quickly. It was a sobering and salutary experience, and I never want to go through it again.

Minale Tattersfield 30 years of Graphic Revolution 1964 1994

Poster for our 30th anniversary. It coincided with the start of the recession.

But despite it all, I believe that the recession was a marvellous thing for the design business. Just as food rationing during the war created a healthier nation and fighting for survival strengthened the British character, so the design industry has emerged from recession leaner, fitter and stronger in spirit. The boom-to-bust scenario of design in Britain is summed up for me by that phoney BT piper symbol whose emergence coincided with the crash. Today we are all playing a new tune in design: it is no longer a question of how the piper looks, it is how the piper performs that matters. Only performance is rewarded.

BT logo designed by Wolff Olins

IDLE HANDS MAKE FALSE WORK

Horror stories about what happened to designers in the recession are now recounted by seasoned campaigners with the same intensity as old soldiers talk about the war. I have plenty of my own. But I also have a theory as to why the design business was hit so hard, especially by the epidemic known as free pitching. Never in the history of design have so many firms chased so few genuine projects. Most jobs were entirely fictitious, invented by idle corporate hands. Let me explain.

The recession left many brand and marketing managers with no budgets, nothing to do all day, and fearful for their jobs. To justify their position within the company, they would instigate a fictitious project, screen up to 20 design groups (remember they've got lots of free time), invite free design proposals, and then present them to their boss. When the boss surveyed all this creative work and asked, "how much did this cost?", the manager was able to proudly announce: "Not a penny, sir". Thus junior brand and marketing managers indulged in a bit of self-promotion on the back of the design business, casting themselves as cost-effective innovators generating new ideas while pushing design consultants to the wall.

One client in Leeds invited no less than 62 different design firms to pitch for a boutique project, an act of total madness which summed up the darkest days of the slump. Another client offered a four-page leaflet to ten different consultants. This kind of behaviour even spread from the UK to Europe. We were invited to Brussels by an automotive client to discuss a project. When we realised it entailed a free pitch, we declined to participate and we took the client to court to recover the cost of the airline tickets. On another occasion, we were asked to do free creative proposals for a well-known whisky brand. When we said no, we were told "we don't like your attitude."

Throughout the business, designers were being insulted on a regular basis. The supermarket chains – notorious for their exploitation of young designers – were among the worst. Sainsbury's even cheekily introduced a scheme whereby designers would return their fees to the client at the end of the year in return for being included on the roster of consultants.

A healthy design for Tesco, for an unhealthy design fee.

BAN FREE PITCHING

Things got so bad that I decided to take a stand. Free pitching was eroding all our self-respect as a profession and turning designer against designer. So I started Minale Tattersfield's now-famous campaign in Britain, entitled Ban Free Pitching. We took full-page advertisements in *Design Week* to launch our initiative and solicit signatures of support. The response was fantastic – more than a thousand replies, not just from all over the UK but from mainland Europe too. And not just design firms either but also clients. I was particularly gratified by the response of British Gas. "If you were one of the consultancies that didn't insult my intelligence by offering speculative design services," wrote British Gas Exhibitions manager David Wise, "your brochure/letter will be kept on file, and should a suitable opportunity present itself I will contact you."

As I explained earlier in this book, participating in speculative unpaid pitches is more dangerous for designers than playing Russian roulette. Fortunately we were able to mobilise the entire design industry and although the problem of free pitching has not gone away, at last the dangers have been suitably highlighted. Also now that the recession has abated somewhat, there are less idle corporate hands to make mischief with fictitious design projects. Those managers have either been sacked or they at last have real work to do.

THE BUREAUCRATIC BURDEN

Erica Jong, author of *Fear of Flying*, once wrote: "The trouble is, if you don't risk anything, you risk even more." But the sad truth is that recession makes people more conservative, not more daring. It certainly knocked the seat-of-the-pants risk element right out of design and introduced the age of form-filling and box-ticking. The Bureaucratic burdens placed on designers in recent times have been incredible. We were recently invited by BAA plc, the former British Airports Authority, to sign up for its BAA Preferred Supplier Programme as it was looking at design services to be commissioned over the next five years. We received a giant 44-page questionnaire which must have taken many trees to produce, asking us to answer the most complex, intensive and irrelevant series of questions I have ever seen. This was the form to end all forms and would have taken months to fill in. It gave me a distinct 'fear of flying' with BAA!

It was all the more galling as we had enjoyed an extensive track record of working for BAA over many years. But that didn't seem to count – only the Bureaucratic task of form-filling seemed to be important. So I wrote BAA this letter: "We would still like to be part of the BAA design team considering that our collaboration with BAA has lasted almost 25 years, but alas, the task of completing the questionnaire is above our capabilities. On the other hand we are very capable of designing trains, rail stations, underground stations, signage systems etc etc..."

By following the Bureaucratic box-ticking route in trying to differentiate between design firms, I believe BAA will end up with a roster of consultancies who are good at talking about design, but not at doing it. Describing design ability is not the same as doing it, and the ability to fill in forms is not the same as the ability to design things. Those who are often best at design are often the worst at describing the process. And vice versa. It is a bit like asking a top novelist to do a painting of his novel using 12 colours on a canvas and then judging the quality of the novel on the painting alone.

A STANDARD TORMENT

Another Bureaucratic burden which presented itself to designers in the recession was a real torment – the quality standard BS 5750. This was another product of too many people with too much time on their hands during the slump. Not only did we have to contend with falling workloads, frozen budgets and incessant demands to fill in endless forms or make free pitches to win work – we were pestered by clients, especially Government clients, saying that failure to comply with BS 5750 would cost us business. It was torture, but I was certain of one thing. Application for BS 5750 was the one sure-fire way to go bankrupt. So we didn't do it.

I knew that BS 5750 would make us less, not more, efficient. I knew it would take up precious staff hours to comply. I knew it was totally irrelevant to the design business. I knew that clients insistent on BS 5750 accreditation would not pay proper fees anyway. So we stuck to our guns. And what do we see today? BS 5750 is fading from the scene. Now that everyone is busier, the bureaucrats are in retreat. Those design firms who bothered to get BS 5750 now find it is meaningless in practical terms. Big clients don't give a damn about it. A recent commission from London Transport confirms my point. Twenty years ago, we were asked to look at the Oval Underground Station. Today we are redesigning it. We didn't have BS 5750 then. We don't have BS 5750 now.

The Oval underground station.
First proposal in 1975.

Final solution 1995

The cricket ball shown in 1975
is now here!

STAYING ALIVE

In the recession, we needed to forgo the luxuries and pull in the belt to survive. That, of course, was anathema to my culture. I'm a true Italian when it comes to not under-spending on art and design. As I read recently: "Who but an Italian, Pope Pius II, could congratulate his architect, Bernardo Rosselino, for overspending on the cathedral and palace of Piacenza? 'You did well, Bernado, in lying to us about the expense'." Still, we had no choice. We were close to the edge and watched many design firms with high overheads and an unhealthy ratio of sales people to designers topple over the edge. We badly needed commissions, but so many of the jobs were frustratingly fictitious. On one occasion I went with my Italian agent to a meeting in Milan with an advertising agency to discuss a packaging project for an unnamed client (it turned out to be Alfa Romeo). We wanted to know everything about the project but the client didn't want to tell us anything. The advertising agency played its cards very close to its chest, saying "consider this a platonic love affair." Sensing a protracted courting period with no real outcome, my agent asked plaintively, "Couldn't we make love ?" The advertising agency replied, "If we have to make love, then it's only a question of money!" Of course nothing was consummated. There was no real job at the end of it.

But even when projects were genuine, we sometimes missed out on them. The British Gas corporate identity programme, one of few big projects around at the time, was a case in point. We fell foul of that old problem – presenting to the board after a heavy lunch. Remember how we missed out on the refurbishment of Unilever House back in 1982? The same thing happened with

British Gas. We were on a final shortlist after winning through
from an initial list of 15 firms. Coley Porter Bell presented
at 11.00am. We presented at 2.30pm. Our solutions were
coincidentally identical – a gas flame encased within a globe.
Coley Porter Bell won the job. We didn't. British Gas chief
executive Cedric Brown – he of the controversial pay packet –
slept soundly through our presentation. Presumably he'd stayed
awake for Coley Porter Bell! Such is life.

Our first credential presentation to British Gas.

Our second presentation.

Final solution by Coley Porter Bell.

But you can't always blame the organisers of design presentations to the board for disappointments. The big problem is that nobody has scientifically proved the business effectiveness of design, enabling the old adage "in a boom you don't need it, in a recession you can't afford it" to hold sway. There are always other factors and marketing disciplines – from timing of launch and market conditions to advertising and public relations campaigns – which influence the performance of any new design. It is very difficult to freeze-frame the design input, to isolate the particular contribution that design makes.

I know that we now have the Design Effectiveness Awards in the UK which seek to do precisely that. But I think such awards are a waste of time. They just show that some design firms have executives with time on their hands to collect all the facts and figures needed for an entry. Really effective and successful design firms are usually too busy to fill in all the forms. We produce design that doubles the sales, but to put down all the information that explains why the sale has doubled will take us longer than to produce the design!

Crown Jewel premium gin.
A great international sales success
for our client James Borrough,
1994. It was never entered for
the Design Effectiveness Awards.
Where you can write 3000 words
on a single design! I challenge
Shakespeare to do so!

THE GUARDIAN
Tuesday November 2 1993

It was meant to be the brave new face of London Underground, but the grim Centre West in Hammersmith is unlikely to improve its image

The monster in the west

Deyan Sudjic

*The article in The Guardian **by** Deyan Sudjic.*

PERSPECTIVES

Minale Tattersfield has cleaned up at west London's busiest underground station, says Liz Farrelly

All change at Hammersmith

*The Blueprint article **edited** by Deyan Sudjic.*

MEDIA FOCUS

DESIGN MAGAZINES

Title	Publisher	Frequency	Cover price	Circulation	% change	Comment
Blueprint	*(illegible)*	*(illegible)*				
Creative Review	Centaur Communications	Monthly	£2.50	15,718	-8	Looks desperately old
Design	Design Council	Monthly				*(illegible)*
Design Week	Centaur Communications	Weekly	£3.95	8,702	-13	Has not fulfilled its potential
XYZ	Haymarket Magazines	Monthly				
FX	ETP	Bi-monthly	£4.00	33,750	N/A	-

Designer points of reference

Who reads design magazines? After 30 years in the design profession, the only answer is: I don't know!

Designers are strange animals, usually interested only in themselves. From time to time, they actually read a design magazine, but only when they, or a competitor, are featured. On the positive side, they will never chuck away a design title, but will file it in the corner of some office on the off-chance that it will be needed as reference or for copying something.

Design is the most glorious of the four mainstream design titles selected. Newly redesigned, the magazine fits the trend towards making magazines look mid-50s, and it has succeeded admirably.

The contents are always mildly interesting, because it is a Design Council publication and so the political angle — designer versus industry — is regurgitated almost ad nauseam.

However, *Design* is part of the British design tradition, having been around since 1949 when the word "design" was conceived in its modern sense. It speaks with a certain amount of authority as the number one reference magazine in the UK for the design industry.

The advertising is a mix of furniture manufacturer, car technology and paper merchant, but, thank God, not "graphic computer technology" yet.

Design covers too many areas of the design industry superficially and none deeply, and this is a problem for advertisers which, by nature, like to be focused. The classified section, being monthly, lacks the feeling of urgency that readers usually require.

Design Week has not fulfilled

Marcello Minale upholds a tradition and flicks quickly through the design press

Design publications...for reference

its potential because the news it carries is not news. This is because when a design company wins an important design assignment, the client does not want it to divulge the news and the design company does not want to divulge the source of the win.

So *Design Week* is full of no news, or news of no consequence. Let's face it, what news is "CSD mulls over snub by Denton" or "Inland Revenue trawls for talent"? Pity, because I believe *Design Week* is the only weekly the design professional actually reads. I also like the "non" style and presentation.

The classified section is a must for the industry, although the display has problems (like all the design press) and is a mish-mash of badly designed and badly presented ads.

Creative Review is the design

magazine that traditionally is flicked through as fast as possible. Unfortunately, this is now more difficult due to all the different types of paper and inserts. I think *Creative Review* has lost its way. It started well with good intentions, but has developed into a mumble jumble of visual tight-rope exercises and it looks desperately old.

The advertising is split into two categories — paper manufacturers and advertising awards sponsored by paper manufacturers. The square format must cause adaptation problems for every art director. However, I did spot one, Nikon's "sharpen up your image", which was adapted and still retained its punch.

Blueprint has sentimental value for me, having witnessed its birth in the basement of our old studio in Putney. The format size is excellent and the layout is first class, even if slightly dated, but I am sure it will evolve soon.

The contents: when it sticks to architecture it has great authority; where it dabbles into other areas such as fashion, graphics, textiles, or illustration, it misfires badly.

I have to confess I have never read an article in *Blueprint*, but with such visuals you don't need to read the text — it spoils your first impression and your judgment.

The ads are all of good design and the size a feast for the art director. It seems furniture and lighting manufacturers have found what they did not find in *Design*, and they pour in fast and furious.

Marcello Minale is the chairman of Minale Tattersfield Design Strategy Group and is a past president of the Designers' and Art Directors' Association

The culprit! The Campaign article by Marcello Minale.

PUBLICITY IS A DOUBLE-EDGED SWORD

The recession provided me with an immediate and largely unwelcome opportunity to revisit all the advice I had given to young design entrepreneurs earlier in this book. I resolved to practice what I had preached, especially when it came to keeping the public relations momentum going despite the bad times. When we completed the design of the new Hammersmith Underground Station – the first major architectural project by a graphics-based group – I thought we had a golden opportunity for some good press. It turned into a gigantic disaster.

Deyan Sudjic, *The Guardian's* influential architectural critic, slammed the scheme. And I mean slammed it. Under the headline "The monster in the west", Sudjic wrote: "This was meant to be the brave new face of London Underground. But despite Minale Tattersfield's credentials, they have produced a nightmarish environment of harsh lights, crude tiles, of spaces devoid of quality, of finishes stripped of subtlety, delicacy and delight." He regarded the scheme as irritating and self-indulgent, which was all the more disappointing since his own magazine *Blueprint* had already given Hammersmith Station ("Minale Tattersfield has gone for a clean, refined look") the thumbs up. Why had Sudjic come down so hard on the project in *The Guardian*? I think I may know the reason. I cannot be sure, but just weeks before I had foolishly reviewed the design press in the advertising trade paper *Campaign*. I wrote in my review: "I have to confess I have never read an article in *Blueprint*, but with such visuals you don't need to read the text." Now we're all human and no journalist likes to hear that his copy isn't being read. Let me tell Deyan, I certainly read his copy in *The Guardian* !

FALLING OFF THE PYRAMID

During the recession I got out and about around Europe. With more time on my hands I gave lectures to design organisations in Denmark and Ireland, relaying news of the savage culling in the UK design industry. As I saw it, the axings and redundancies didn't reduce the competition. It quadrupled the competition. The day after you sacked a designer, he or she became your competitor. But there was also an upside as top people in the industry were abruptly shown the door.

When the transport division of Addison, a large multi-disciplinary design firm, folded, I swiftly called the experienced architect and designer Maurice Acton, who had worked on the BP and Shell petrol station revamps. The result was the formation of a new alliance and a new company, Minale, Tattersfield & Acton, which specialises in designing petrol stations. The venture has proved successful. We are working for BP, Shell, Repsol, Thai Oil, Agip, IP, and others.

It shows that the topsy-turvy world of recession oddly enough throws up more than its share of new opportunities for business development, but you need to be alert and seize them while you can.

I have this theory that the design business is a stepped and inverted pyramid . Unless you keep stepping up to the next level every two years or so then you get out of step and can fall off. At the bottom of the pyramid, there are lots of small projects, book jackets and the like, and you don't have far to fall. At the top of the pyramid, there are very few large projects – giant identity or architectural projects, for example – and there is a long way to fall. Mess up one project at this level and you can go broke overnight. I know this because we teetered on the edge many times.

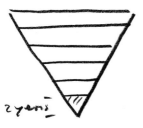

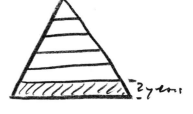

Value of projects increases
every two years (on average).

Number of projects decreases
every two years (on average).

INTO ALIEN TERRITORY

To stabilise the business and beat the recession, we decided that we would export our way out of the crisis. We had already built up an international network in the good times. Now we began to expand into new and decidedly different markets: the Czech Republic, Slovakia, Russia, Poland, Thailand. Sometimes we were lucky, often we were not. It was always different and sometimes weird. But we had to try because we really had little choice.

We enjoyed major success with a series of mobile petrol stations designed as part of Italian petrol company Agip's foray into the Russian market. But we were less successful in Prague where we opened an office in partnership with a rich Czech property magnate. We learnt a big lesson from the experience – never do business with a rich partner.

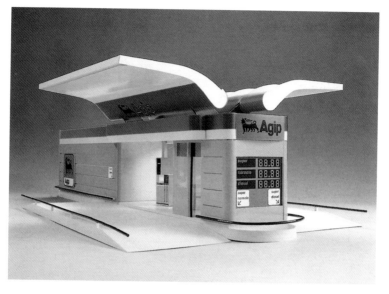

Mobile petrol station for Russia.

In recent history I would say there have been three key events in which people have made money literally overnight – the Gold Rush, the Industrial Revolution and the collapse of Communism. In Prague, many Czech state officials, who barely had their tram fare home, amassed enormous fortunes in a very short time by purchasing former state enterprises for nothing and then selling them to western interests for millions in cash six months later. My new Prague partner fell into that category. But his luxurious image was to prove my undoing in trying to win a packaging design programme from the Promil dairy company in the Czech Republic. He lent me a car, a Mercedes 600SL, and a chauffeur when I paid a visit to the dairy. When the client saw me arriving in a car worth three times the value of the dairy itself, there was no way I was going to be given the commission.

Another Czech project — for the makers of the Tamara early-warning radar system — also ended in tears. The client, Tesla Pardubice, asked Minale Tattersfield to market the system to a wide international audience with a new corporate identity. We worked for 18 months on this fascinating project but we never got paid. The client offered us a Tamara system (value £5 million) to put in our back garden, but we declined to accept this most generous offer. The design business may be ultra-competitive but we have no use yet for radar. We are now pursuing our fees through the courts, but despite its scale and its 3,000 employees, this company apparently has no western cash. We haven't given up on the Czechs, however. We may have parted company with our rich partner but we are convinced this is a market which will pay off eventually, even if the very thought of landing at Prague airport still gives me the shakes. Before one of my first trips there, I received this reassuring fax from a contact at the Leo Burnett agency: "We look forward to meeting you soon and I wish you a pleasant flight as the landing conditions in Prague are terrible."

THE ENGLISH COLLEGE IN PRAGUE

A CRAZY WORLD

Recession always brings complete political, financial, economic and social turmoil. So venturing into new, uncharted design markets was always likely to be a hazardous undertaking. Even so, after opening an office in Kuwait just weeks before Saddam Hussein's army decided to invade the country and the Gulf War broke out, I could have expected slightly better luck. Not a bit of it. When we were asked to design a new corporate identity for Ferruzzi Finanziaria, part of the large Italian conglomerate Gruppo Ferruzzi, we discovered that 50 Ferruzzi managers had been sent to jail as part of the great Italian bribes scandal, known as *tangentopoli*. When we opened an office in Kuala Lumpur to service Malaysian and other Asia Pacific interests, we ran straight into the Anglo-Malaysian trade rift in the wake of the Pergau dam financial fiasco.

Ferruzzi

Montedison

Ferruzzi Finanziaria.
The proposed image of
the two corporations.

Sometimes you just can't win. But whatever happens, you mustn't give up. The Malaysian office has actually borne fruit in an unexpected area: a group of Malaysian businessmen want to open a private art and design school in alliance with Minale Tattersfield, and they are currently raising the £5 million needed to get the project off the ground. Who would have thought of it? A Minale Tattersfield Design College in the Far East. But that's the recession for you. It throws the most unexpected opportunities in your direction, bringing its share of ecstasy as well as agony. As the best-selling American business guru Tom Peters observed: "Crazy times call for crazy organisations." It guarantees never a dull moment, but to hang on in any recession takes nerves of steel.

The promotion is carried on despite the recession, this time in Pescara.

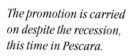

*Minale, Tattersfield Design is sponsoring Luigi Listorti and Cristina Zecca
at the world championship of catamaran HOB 18 in Dubai.*

*Wade Hall-Craggs, with trophy, after winning the Thames World
Sculling Challenge, London, 1993. Picture: Sunday Express*

*We, at Minale Tattersfield, have always believed in sponsorship.
We had some lucky scoops in the national press and television.*

Steve Redgrave, three times olympic champion, trying to be the first sportsman to win four Olympic medals in Atlanta 1996, with the Minale Tattersfield (The Tideway Scullers) winning senior squad at Peterborough Regata, 1995.

Ealing borough junior football team.

British sculling squad training in Lake Cassin, Provence, France.

THE DAY I WAS TOO SICK TO GO TO WORK BY MARCELLO MINALE (JR).

Monday morning, 8.30. I got on my bike for the start of another "manic Monday". I felt a little bored with life, so I decided to take the longer route to work, via the River (strange how the sight of water can give you that up-lifting feeling!).I got to Putney Bridge, where I saw an incredible thing: it was a 37 metre long replica of an ancient Greek warship. It was called the 'Olympias' and it was moored off Putney Pier. I thought to myself that this was the mother of all rowing boats and I must have a go. I got off my bike and approached a group of 'rowing like' people chatting away.

"Jesus, what is this thing doing here?"

I said to one fellow; he turned and without any hesitation and with an enthusiastic American accent said:

"Gee, that ain't any ol'thing, that there is a gen-u-wine Trireme, and me and another 170 oarsmen and women are gonna row that mother from here to the houses of your little Ol'Parliament to cel-e-brate 2500 years of Greek Democracy".

"Wow" I gasped, "and when are you leaving?" (notice how this is slowly turning into a cheap novel. . .).

"Oh, around 9.30, that is if we can get everyone here in time".

At that point my brain was travelling faster than my limited work ethics, and before I could get back on my bike to carry on with my journey to work, I had schemed up a plan that would liven up this dull and dreamy Monday morning. At 9 o'clock I was back home and on the phone to work. I was groaning and moaning to the Secretary, throwing in some Italian words here and there to dramatise the whole affair (in short I told her to tell the boss I had the 'runs' and I couldn't leave the bog seat).

OK: Plan A seemed to have worked, so, back to the River for Plan B. It was 9.30 when I got back to the moored Olympias and a queue of 170 had gathered in my absence. I couldn't help thinking, like most who were there, why it is so hard to get everyone down on time when you are having an outing in an 'eight'. After my cynical thought, I joined the queue and boarded, where I was welcomed with a soft cushion and some instructions on seating from Boris Rankov, one of the trireme organisers.

The word trireme means 'three oars' in Latin, and this was an obvious name for the vessel. It had three rowing decks (the ultimate in ancient ship technology).

The oarsmen on the third deck were called 'Thryonites' (meaning 'third level'). They were the eyes for the men rowing in the lower decks and they had to make sure that each stroke was in unison with them. But there was a price to pay for having a beautiful view: the rowing stroke would be very short, cramped and awkward, since their blades were the furthest from the water.

The second level oarsmen were called 'Zyghians'. Their stroke was a little easier with more room to row, but their bladework had to be very precise. One mistake and they would get caught in between the top and bottom level oars, sending the other rowers into a frenzy of entangled blades (May I add here, this was proved with great success during our outing). The last and bottom level was the engine room. With the blades closest to the water and the draw even and level, it was the truest and most comfortable position to row in. But they too had to pay for their comfort by sitting in total stale, darkness.

I got my seat as a 'Thryonite', with the view, the fresh air and the awkward rowing position. It was rather uncomfortable for everyone, for the ship had been built to the smaller measurements of the average person 2,500 years ago. When we were all cramped in, organised and ready to go, we set off down the river.

For the first ten minutes at least we must have looked like a drunk centipede. After a while as we started to 'catch' on, something quite curious started to happen. The two rowing sides divided by a large gap in the middle started to drift into two different rhythms, this made it very difficult to steer in a straight line. To correct this, Boris shouted out the rhythm, so to bring back both sides rowing together. This didn't work because half the boat in the bows couldn't hear him Since the trireme was built by a group of historians, naval architects and rowing enthusiasts to discover how the ancient Greeks' greatest war machine worked, they had to maintain authenticity, and hadn't cheated by installing some sort of a super large cox-box.

Since no one is sure how the ancient masters stayed synchronised, we tried everything from drums to singing. Our final solution to the problem and probably that of the ancient Greeks was communal humming. At first I couldn't stop laughing at the thought of 170 Buddhist monks rowing and chanting together. But humming worked extremely well and the boat truly became one in spirit and soul.

We tried all sorts of exercises to get us in the mood to test the vessel's ramming speed and manoeuvrability. During the many famous naval battles described in ancient texts, the Trireme would ram the enemy ships, piercing a hole below the waterline and then make a run for it. They escaped after ramming by turning round on their seats, so they would be facing the opposite direction from when they started; they would then grab hold of the man's oar who was previously behind, and row out from the enemy fire in reverse. Once safe, they would reassume their original seating and make a quick 180 degree turn and row back home, leaving a sinking enemy ship, three times its size, in its wake. The ship also carried a handful of fully armed men on the top deck, above the oarsmen, to protect the ship while in its stationary phase between the ram and the reverse out. This vessel was truly the terror of the whole Persian fleet!

These exercises were fun, even if at times they were a real mess: heads banging, oar handles being rammed into your kidneys from behind and groups of blades catching massive communal crabs... While doing these exercises I couldn't help, but admire what these ancient masters of the oar could do under the stress and chaos of battle. They had to stay calm while all around them must have been hell.

With further rowing and confidence building with every stroke and hum, we achieved a top speed of 10 knots (11.5 mph) with the tide. Further trials suggested that for the maximum power the 170 ancient Greeks would have had to row at about 47 strokes a minute. That means dog fights would have had to be over in 10 minutes because that was the period a crew could have rowed at near maximum strength. The trials also showed a maximum range of about 200 miles. The main limiting factor was water: a 200 mile journey would have required at least 800 gallons of water weighting almost four tons.

At 6 pm we moored back at Putney Pier, we pulled in our oars, removed our sore bums from the wooden seats and started to disembark. As we got off, we were supposed to return our cushions to Boris. As I gave him mine, I thanked him for the marvellous day I had, and wondered if, by any chance, he still had some of those T-shirts with the Trireme printed on, left to give away...I had noticed that the whole crew was wearing one. He asked me why

I didn't have one and I answered because nobody had given me one. He then asked if I had paid my subscription fee, and then it hit me between the eyes: I had boarded the 'Olympias' clandestinely. Feeling embarrassed and wanting to vanish there and then, I replied in a squeaky voice:

"Yes, of course I have!".

He looked straight at me and said:

"Oh, well, sorry about the T-shirt, here's one extra".

He gave it to me and told me that they were leaving half an hour earlier the next day. I nodded OK, took the T-shirt and left very briskly.

To make a short story long, needless to say, at 9 o'clock the next morning I was not at Putney Pier, but entering the front door at work. From the moment I got in, to the time I got upstairs four people had asked me if I was feeling any better from my stomach attack. I replied I was, thank you, and thought how strange it was that never before had I received so much sympathy for being ill and off work. When I arrived at my desk everything became clear; a copy of The Independent was spread open with this photo of me peering out of the 'Olympias', looking rather healthy and well. A little later I was told that the boss had seen it, read it, put it on my desk, got on his motorbike and was off to Putney to get a row in the Trireme as well.

P.S. I'd like to add (if the boss is reading), that I have matured and that my work ethics are much higher now. And that the Trireme won't be back for a long time. Cheers.

Picture: The Independent

CHAPTER TEN

GOING INTERACTIVE – CREATIVITY IN THE COMPUTER AGE

GOING INTERACTIVE

CREATIVITY IN THE COMPUTER AGE

When I started out in the design business, the technology involved was relatively simple and straightforward. Even when I first wrote about my formative experiences in this book, the technology was only in transition and some of the old, familiar tools remained. But today the technology used in designing has changed beyond all recognition. We have entered the era of multimedia, of interactivity, and who knows where it will all end.

The emergence of the computer has been the biggest single change of the past five years. The computer has not only revolutionised the way designers work, it has revolutionised the way they think. Not all change is necessarily for the better, but in the spirit of embracing the new, we have launched a new venture entitled Minale Tattersfield Interactive. The consultancy symbolised by a pencil scribble has gone digital – naturally, the logo for the new company turns the Scribble trademark into a computer mouse mat.

The decision whether to become involved in this new market was a hard one to make. It made us confront some of the most basic truths about the medium in which we work and the skills we use. You can look at the multimedia market in two ways, rather like the two shoe salesmen who went to Africa and one said "here's a great market – everyone is barefoot", and the other one replied "not a chance – nobody wears shoes". On the one hand, there is virgin territory to be conquered – much untapped potential. On the other hand, people are largely unaware of that potential and could very well live happily without it.

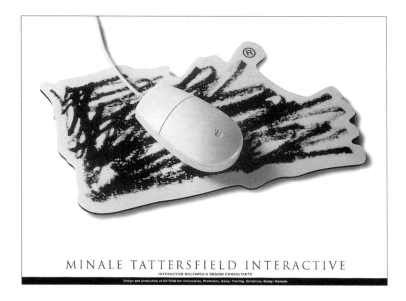

MINALE TATTERSFIELD INTERACTIVE

INTERACTIVE MULTIMEDIA DESIGN CONSULTANTS

Design and production of CD ROM for: Information, Promotion, Sales, Training, Exhibition, Design Manuals

I believe that multimedia technology is in search of a market to justify the millions of dollars spent on researching it. This is a technology imposed by its makers rather than one developed in answer to a pressing need. If you look at leading-edge multimedia projects, the clients are always telecommunications companies desperate to find an application for their invention. Like the Hovercraft in relation to the boat, electronic communication is a solution to a problem which didn't really exist.

The traditional print medium has still got a lot going for it. You can pick up and read a brochure or a book in one movement. It takes two movements to insert a disk and boot up a computer. If you innovate so that you move from two movements to one movement − if you reduce and simplify − you can be guaranteed of success. But if you move from one movement to two movements, aren't you courting failure? That feeling is at the back of my mind. Nevertheless we have decided to take the plunge with Minale Tattersfield Interactive on the grounds that even if it is a giant flop and the entire multimedia industry a complete whitewash, then at least we will fail with a clear conscience because we gave it a go.

I am, however, reassured by the words of the advertising guru Winston Fletcher who recently wrote that design companies are likely to create the best interactive communications because such firms are "best at providing information and options" in brochures, catalogues, direct marketing and so on. "In old-fashioned jargon," explained Fletcher, "interactive communications are more likely to be found below the mythical line than above it."

INFORMATION, NOT ENTERTAINMENT

To set up Minale Tattersfield Interactive, we have brought in experts in multimedia and interactive design to work with us to develop the new service. New technology extends the dimensions of graphic design. It is no longer just a case of the static dimensions of height, width, depth, proportion. Sound, movement and interactivity must be considered. But I don't see why a graphic designer can't also handle the moving image and be a movie director. It is simply a case of learning to master new tools, which designers have always done.

At the heart of it all, there must be a human being with a brain directing the communications. Up to now, the trouble is that computer-generated graphics have been treated as a branch of electronic engineering and have consequently been a total visual and perceptual disaster. I admire the New York visionary of digital communications, Robert M Greenberg, who said: "On the network you'd better have a person somewhere who has a vision, or the work will just be crap. It's not going to communicate, it's not going to get anyone to transact, it's not going to be profitable. It'll just be a hodge-podge."

I am consequently very clear about what the main applications and benefits of interactive communications are likely to be. The focus should be on information, not entertainment. How can a computer disk beat a book or a trip to the cinema on an entertainment level? Computer programmes kill all fantasy – and you have to give people scope for their own imagination. Personally, I think there is no contest between playing tennis on a computer and playing tennis on a real grass court. Who wants their kids to spend each and every night surfing the Internet for three hours at a time?

However, the data storage of CD-ROM creates new opportunities in the presentation of information that users can interrogate. Sending a university prospectus on CD-ROM to students with access to a computer is a worthwhile development. And remember that as computers reduce and reduce in size and price, they will eventually become as ubiquitous as propelling pencils.

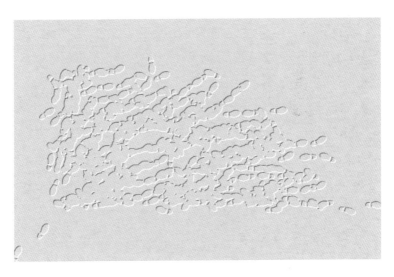

Our latest Christmas card, 1995; still produced by hand!!

So Minale Tattersfield Interactive will focus on such areas as information catalogues, staff training aids, design manuals and exhibition displays where people can access data at their own speed and use the system to suit their own requirements. We want to create interactive communications which are simpler, richer, more friendly, and that will take a lot of thought, not simply a lot of megabytes. The whole computer environment is currently driving the design industry into a complete frenzy because it turns the designer into typesetter, compositor, proof reader and much else besides. This was symbolised for me by a Hellman cartoon in *Design Week* in which a designer – bog-eyed from staring at the screen too much – talks gibberish about being an Internet guru... and a teapot!

There is also a great deal of mystifying Web-Net-style jargon associated with computers. But then designers should be used to jargon having lived with printers for so long. If you're having a hard time keeping up with computers and think wistfully back to the good old days, just remember all that dreadful print jargon. Remember too that our biggest enemy was often not the client but the printer who would sit in meetings and say, "You can't print that!" Once, in 1975, I was presenting a packaging solution for the Schweppes Russian tonic brand to the client's agency, Saatchi & Saatchi. The printer raised constant objections. I asked him to leave the room with me and we returned ten minutes later to announce that everything was resolved. The job would be printed the way I had specified. Nobody knew how we had managed to reach an agreement. Now 20 years later, I can reveal the truth. I took him into a room next door, forced him into a corner and, being a fit oarsman, I threatened the poor man with

violence if he didn't comply! Computer technology may have its drawbacks but there were frustrations with the old ways of doing things too.

INTERRUPTING THE DESIGN PROCESS

A lot of people have asked me whether the new technology has in some way diminished creative standards in graphic design. I have to say that, frankly, the answer is yes. I blame two key tools of the trade which have grown ever more sophisticated over the past five years: the Apple Macintosh and the photo library. Both tools have come to dominate the conceptual starting point of projects when they should simply be providing the means of execution.

In the days before the Macintosh, designers would think about a solution and then find a way to execute that idea. Today that vital thinking period has been lost. Designers go immediately to the Macintosh and do their thinking on screen. It used to be 'think – then do'. Now it is 'start doing and moving things around and it'll all come right in the end'. The computer has affected the mannerisms of design. It is meant to be a tool of execution but it has interfered with the very process of design thinking. The result has been a lot of uninspired solutions. The rise of the photo library hasn't helped either. Again, designers in the old days would think up a solution first and then find a way to execute it. Now they scramble for those stock image catalogues which have 20 different varieties of every conceivable shape, situation and texture. Projects start not by thinking but by looking in the photo library catalogues for inspiration.

AUNTIE GLUG MECHANISM

MA TOMATO

PAR KWAY

GRAN GELATO

Cartoons still drawn by hand regularly appear on our notice board. In this case by Steve Aldridge from our interior design division.

Some designers are now beginning to react against the trend of the computer controlling the concept and I say good luck to them. They are claiming 'designed by hand' as a badge of virtue whereas ten years ago they were claiming 'designed by computer'. As Arthur C Clarke once said: " The future is not what it used to be!" The craft of hot metal printing is back and there is open revolt against the computer in some sections of the design community.

The trouble with the computer is that it provides us with too many options. So designers in turn give the client too many options. I have already stated in this book that you are lucky if you find one solution that is right for the client, not 75 solutions. I don't think the cause of the client, or the designer, is well served by producing a sheer quantity of solutions on computer. It is best to provide one solution, maybe counterpointed by one alternative. But the computer has turned design into a game of 'never mind the quality, feel the width'.

The computer has also enabled designers to compose such incredible, exceptional images that very little surprises or shocks us any more. Thirty years ago I remember seeing a photograph of 2,000 people with ambulances in a desert, part of a Royal Insurance campaign. I thought it was a wonderful shot because it was so difficult to achieve. Today a similar shot would not amaze, it would not be exceptional, because people would automatically think it had been composed digitally. It has become far harder for designers to solicit genuine emotional response through imagery. The ability to surprise and amaze people has diminished dramatically. It is like, the further people push the frontiers of eroticism, the less people are really shocked.

Computers enable us to do things easily that were once all but impossible to achieve. To prove my point, at Minale Tattersfield we recently produced on computer 264 different numeric logotypes in a single afternoon as folios for a book. As the skill of doing things in design is lessened by technology, as anyone with access to a computer can scream as loud as they like, then the only way to get noticed in the future will be to use total silence.

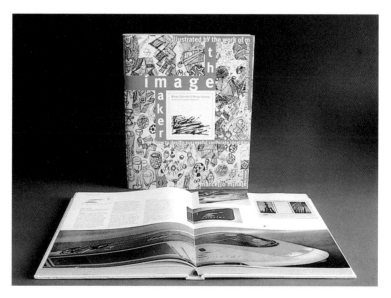

Our latest book on corporate identities published by Edward Booth-Clibborn.

The poster promoting "The Image Maker".
All the numbers were produced on computer.

Thirty years ago, it was a revelation to see the less-is-more, modernist graphics gurus putting small black squares on white paper. Today it may again be a revelation to see....the less-is-more, modernist graphics gurus putting small black squares on white paper.

Then there is the fact that the computer has enabled designers to desktop publish smart reports and presentations swiftly and easily. This facility has encouraged an unhealthy obsession with words, planning, strategy and unnecessary rationalisations of the design. It is the cancer of the profession, so much so that the creative phase of the job is compressed and the more rubbish you write at the outset, the better your chances of winning a big job.

Today "Quack, quack" is the cancer of the profession.

Cartoon by Larson

In fact, winning the job is now all that matters in the design industry. Design firms used to spend ten per cent of their energy winning the job and 90 per cent of their energy designing it. Now it is 90 per cent winning the job and 10 per cent designing it. By the time the commission has been tortuously secured after endless reports, many designers have already spent the fee and are completely exhausted. That is why the creative results are so often poor.

LEAVE IT TO THE PEOPLE

You might surmise from all this that I am pessimistic about the future of the design profession. I am not. I simply think that we live in increasingly uncertain times and that the big design groups are dinosaurs who must adapt or they will soon be extinct. I also believe there is plenty of room for individual designers to express their creativity, with or without the computer. The design profession currently is going through the biggest changes since the Industrial Revolution. This is the Information Revolution and I am not too old to be part of it.

I always say that if you leave it to machines it will be disastrous, but if you leave it to people they can be guaranteed to find a way through. So I would like to wish you luck with your own design business and leave you with the next generation. Since the first edition of this book many of the Minale Tattersfied people who helped us get where we are today have had babies. Here are the Minale Tattersfield babies. Remember, our past is our future...

ART CENTER COLLEGE OF DESIGN

(clockwise from top): Kate and Anna Honey (Liza), Charlotte Jones (Diane),
George Carrow (Liz and Pete), Robert McCook (Susan), Emma Unwin (Jon),
Samuel Williams (Julia), Arthur and Henry Blazey (Lucy),
and Anna and Marta Kelsey (Quentin).

THE LAST PAGE...OPPORTUNITY!

The financial story of the decade must be Nick Leeson, the rogue trader, forcing Peter Baring to take early retirement; culprit the infamous account number 88888 and a hole of £800 million!

We have decided to form a company called 88888 financial design!

Imagine the Financial Director's face when they have to issue a payment for work completed to account number 88888. Imagine the Chairman twitching when the Marketing Executive informs him he has appointed 88888 for all their financial design! And the Inland Revenue's joy when they investigate the business of 88888.

A crazy idea? Yes, an opportunity! Time will tell!!

Financial Design

88888

The new logo!